Children in Charge 4

The Participation Rights of the Child
Rights and Responsibilities in Family and Society

Målfrid Grude Flekkøy

Natalie Hevener Kaufman

Jessica Kingsley Publishers
London and Bristol, Pennsylvania

The right of Målfrid Grude Flekkøy and Natalie Hevener Kaufman to be identified as authors of this work has been asserted by them in accordance with the Copyright, Designs and Patents Act 1988.

First published in the United Kingdom in 1997 by
Jessica Kingsley Publishers Ltd
116 Pentonville Road
London N1 9JB, England
and
1900 Frost Road, Suite 101
Bristol, PA 19007, U S A

Copyright © 1997 Målfrid Grude Flekkøy
and Natalie Hevener Kaufman

Library of Congress Cataloging in Publication Data
A CIP catalogue record for this book is available from the Library of Congress

British Library Cataloguing in Publication Data
A CIP catalogue record for this book is available from the British Library

ISBN 1-85302-489-9 hb
ISBN 1-85302-490-2 pb

Printed and Bound in Great Britain by
Athenaeum Press, Gateshead, Tyne & Wear

UNIVERSITY OF
WOLVERHAMPTON
KNOWLEDGE • INNOVATION • ENTERPRISE

Harrison Learning Centre
City Campus
University of Wolverhampton
St Peter's Square
Wolverhampton WV1 1RH
Telephone: 0845 408 1631
Online Renewals:
www.wlv.ac.uk/lib/myaccount

Telephone Renewals: 01902 321333 or 0845 408 1631
Online Renewals: www.wlv.ac.uk/lib/myaccount
Please return this item on or before the last date shown above.
Fines will be charged if items are returned late.
See tariff of fines displayed at the Counter.

Children in Charge series

Children in Charge
The Child's Right to a Fair Hearing
Edited by Mary John
ISBN 1 85302 368 X
Children in Charge 1

Children in Our Charge
The Child's Right to Resources
Edited by Mary John
ISBN 1 85302 369 8
Children in Charge 2

A Charge Against Society
The Child's Right to Protection
Edited by Mary John
ISBN 1 85302 411 2
Children in Charge 3

of related interest

A Voice for Children
Speaking Out as Their Ombudsman
Målfrid Grude Flekkøy
ISBN 1 85302 118 0 pb
ISBN 1 85302 119 9 hb

Dedication

To the children in our lives, most importantly: Carrollee, Athey, Miranda and Jacob, Eirik and Eilev, Kjetil, Renee and Idun, and Ingunn.

Acknowledgements

We extend our heartfelt gratitude to our friends and colleagues at the Institute for Families in Society, University of South Carolina in Columbia, S.C. Most of all our thanks go to the Director of the Institute, Gary Melton, for bringing us together (one from Norway) and giving us the opportunity of working together, and for reading and commenting on our ideas and drafts.

some have special family and/or juvenile courts. Some have well-developed child welfare systems which take care of cases which in other countries are brought to court. All these differences clearly create problems when writing for an international audience. This is not, therefore, a book primarily about law, although some of the legal issues are included and will be used as examples. These examples will be mostly from those two countries best known to the authors – Norway and the USA – two countries which lend themselves to comparison and highlighting of issues because they are so very different.

Previous writing and discussion of the competence of children in relation to self-expression (i.e. giving opinions, freedom of speech, association and religion, participating in and gradually taking over decision-making) has been mainly concerned with children in special situations, such as the child welfare system, courts, or within the health services. Sufficient attention has not been given to ordinary children in everyday situations, focusing on the evolving capacities of the child. Many discussions seem to treat 'children' as if all persons under 18 years of age have the same skills and competencies, regardless of age and experience. Others address concerns of 'young people' 14–18 years old. Evidence of interest in decision-making capacities of very young children has recently appeared (e.g. in Denmark and the UK), and we are also beginning to realize fully how much the competence of children depends on experience as well as maturation. Our main concern, therefore, is to focus on the normal development of ordinary children, to illustrate how children can exercise their self-expression rights from birth onwards. We wish to highlight the importance of self-expression for the healthy development of communities as well as of individuals. Normal families, institutions and environments offer children opportunities for practice, learning and improvement of the culturally and socially acceptable ways to give opinions, make choices and be active participants in the decision-making processes which concern them.

In this book we will not suggest solutions or describe examples pertaining to every imaginable situation in which a child could or should express themselves, state opinions, make choices or share the decision-making. We hope instead to offer some criteria for considering children's self-expression and some practical examples. Our goal is to provide a basis of respect for the child, to offer a mode of thinking which may encourage further debate, and also to provide inspiration for new ways of including children in democratice processes.

Contents

Let us recall that with the Convention on the Rights of the Child, the international community was able, for the first time, to lay a bridge across the ideological gulf that has traditionally separated civil and political rights from economic, social and cultural rights. People forget that. Countries forget it. On occasion – dare I say it – international forums overlook it. But here we have a Convention where all rights are fully integrated. In a word: indivisible…

We believe that the Convention's articles on children's rights to participation and to freedom of belief can be used to strengthen and enrich democracy, both where it is new and fragile and where it is venerable and stable. Although children do not have the right to vote, we all know that children can be powerful agents for social change.

James P. Grant
Address to the World Conference on
Human Rights, Vienna, June 1993

Introduction

The UN Convention on the Rights of the Child was adopted unanimously the UN General Assembly in November 1989 and has, as of May 1996, be acceded to or ratified by 187 nations and signed by 3 (Oman, the USA a Switzerland), leaving 3 uncommitted (Saudi Arabia, United Arab Emirates a Somalia).

In many nations the national constitution will determine that, once ratifie an international convention becomes a part of national law, in which case it c be cited as national law administratively and in the courts. In other countri in order for the convention to be fully implemented, the nation must chan or incorporate the convention provisions into national law. Once ratified, t treaty is binding for external purposes, but in this set of countries internal acti rests on bringing national law into conformity with the requirements of t Convention. In these cases the Convention cannot be applied in the cou although the Convention requirements can have an advisory effect.

National law also differs from country to country, for example in the deg to which legislative measures are used to regulate conditions within the count Apart from the fact that respect for the law differs widely from population population, the goals of legislation may differ. In some countries legislation mainly reactive or prohibitive, in others also proactive or protective. So countries consider legislation an appropriate means of strengthening changi attitudes within the population. (One example is the legislation found in so countries that prohibits even parents from striking their children.) In so nations simple questions may be settled by statutes, laws or regulations, example at what age a child may go to the movies and which films he or s then can attend. In other countries this would be unthinkable.

Some court systems accept cases not accepted in others, such as class acti litigation. In some countries a large number of different types of grievances settled by the courts; in others only very serious problems reach litigation. T systems created in different countries to uphold the law, reactive as well proactive, differ. Some countries have separate courts for penal and civil actio

PART I

The Rationale
for Children's Rights

Contents

Let us recall that with the Convention on the Rights of the Child, the international community was able, for the first time, to lay a bridge across the ideological gulf that has traditionally separated civil and political rights from economic, social and cultural rights. People forget that. Countries forget it. On occasion – dare I say it – international forums overlook it. But here we have a Convention where all rights are fully integrated. In a word: indivisible…

We believe that the Convention's articles on children's rights to participation and to freedom of belief can be used to strengthen and enrich democracy, both where it is new and fragile and where it is venerable and stable. Although children do not have the right to vote, we all know that children can be powerful agents for social change.

James P. Grant
Address to the World Conference on
Human Rights, Vienna, June 1993

Introduction

The UN Convention on the Rights of the Child was adopted unanimously by the UN General Assembly in November 1989 and has, as of May 1996, been acceded to or ratified by 187 nations and signed by 3 (Oman, the USA and Switzerland), leaving 3 uncommitted (Saudi Arabia, United Arab Emirates and Somalia).

In many nations the national constitution will determine that, once ratified, an international convention becomes a part of national law, in which case it can be cited as national law administratively and in the courts. In other countries, in order for the convention to be fully implemented, the nation must change or incorporate the convention provisions into national law. Once ratified, the treaty is binding for external purposes, but in this set of countries internal action rests on bringing national law into conformity with the requirements of the Convention. In these cases the Convention cannot be applied in the courts, although the Convention requirements can have an advisory effect.

National law also differs from country to country, for example in the degree to which legislative measures are used to regulate conditions within the country. Apart from the fact that respect for the law differs widely from population to population, the goals of legislation may differ. In some countries legislation is mainly reactive or prohibitive, in others also proactive or protective. Some countries consider legislation an appropriate means of strengthening changing attitudes within the population. (One example is the legislation found in some countries that prohibits even parents from striking their children.) In some nations simple questions may be settled by statutes, laws or regulations, for example at what age a child may go to the movies and which films he or she then can attend. In other countries this would be unthinkable.

Some court systems accept cases not accepted in others, such as class action litigation. In some countries a large number of different types of grievances are settled by the courts; in others only very serious problems reach litigation. The systems created in different countries to uphold the law, reactive as well as proactive, differ. Some countries have separate courts for penal and civil actions, some have special family and/or juvenile courts. Some have well-developed child welfare systems which take care of cases which in other countries are brought to court. All these differences clearly create problems when writing for an international audience. This is not, therefore, a book primarily about law, although some of the legal issues are included and will be used as examples. These examples will be mostly from those two countries best known to the authors – Norway and the USA – two countries which lend themselves to comparison and highlighting of issues because they are so very different.

Previous writing and discussion of the competence of children in relation to self-expression (i.e. giving opinions, freedom of speech, association and religion, participating in and gradually taking over decision-making) has been mainly concerned with children in special situations, such as the child welfare system, courts, or within the health services. Sufficient attention has not been given to ordinary children in everyday situations, focusing on the evolving capacities of the child. Many discussions seem to treat 'children' as if all persons under 18 years of age have the same skills and competencies, regardless of age and experience. Others address concerns of 'young people' 14–18 years old. Evidence of interest in decision-making capacities of very young children has recently appeared (e.g. in Denmark and the UK), and we are also beginning to realize fully how much the competence of children depends on experience as well as maturation. Our main concern, therefore, is to focus on the normal development of ordinary children, to illustrate how children can exercise their self-expression rights from birth onwards. We wish to highlight the importance of self-expression for the healthy development of communities as well as of individuals. Normal families, institutions and environments offer children opportunities for practice, learning and improvement of the culturally and socially acceptable ways to give opinions, make choices and be active participants in the decision-making processes which concern them.

In this book we will not suggest solutions or describe examples pertaining to every imaginable situation in which a child could or should express themselves, state opinions, make choices or share the decision-making. We hope instead to offer some criteria for considering children's self-expression and some practical examples. Our goal is to provide a basis of respect for the child, to offer a mode of thinking which may encourage further debate, and also to provide inspiration for new ways of including children in democratice processes.

The Rationale
for Children's Rights

CHAPTER ONE

Human Rights in General

PHILOSOPHIES OF RIGHTS

Philosophers have offered many possible explanations for the theory of rights. The Judeo-Christian tradition bases rights on the existence of the individual as a creation of a Supreme Being: a person's soul or spiritual essence entitles each person to fundamental rights. Greek and Roman philosophers argued that rights were associated with the capacity to reason – a capacity only found in the male citizens. Reasoning ability enabled citizens to understand their world and entitled them to a role in making decisions which affected them and protected them from arbitrary governmental harm. Aquinas merged some elements of each of these traditions, arguing that the ability to reason distinguished humans from other creatures. Each person created by God with reasoning ability was entitled to fundamental rights which could not be abridged by worldly powers. People who denied the basic rights of others, he explained, became as beasts, no longer human. Many societies today continue to base the concept of fundamental rights on religious or spiritual grounds. However, there are also functional bases for fundamental rights, particularly in democracies. The assumption of equality of participation in governance requires that access to the benefits of public life extend to all members on an equal basis.

Democratic theory argues for the necessity of an informed and active citizenry. A knowledgeable public is in a position to exercise the vigilance which will keep government, invested with power and responsibility, from exercising their power in a corrupt or exploitative manner. Democratic government is government by the people, and must heed the voice of the people. Democracy would be meaningless if the 'voice of the people' only consisted of the opinion of the government. Democracy therefore assumes that the people are free to voice many opinions. It follows that each member of the population must be educated, and that education must include the development of critical thinking as an important goal. Without an education or the ability to think critically and creatively, people would be unable to evaluate their government and propose alternatives to government action. While inculcation of values that will make good citizens is essential, indoctrination can have no place in a democratic system. Rights such as freedom of assembly, freedom of speech and access to information, including freedom of press, are examples of functional rights, necessary to the proper operation of democracy. Another set of functional rights are those recognized to assure that individuals will not be harmed by an arbitrary government. Rights to life, liberty, fair trial and privacy exemplify this set of rights.

The concept of human rights rests on a basic concern for the protection of the dignity, integrity and equality of the individual as well as for society. When strong elements in a population dominate the weaker, society's need to control becomes a question of the degree to which control of the individual is necessary in order that society might function. It becomes clear that there is a need to limit expression of the individual in respect to other individuals. As will be discussed later (see Chapter Two), other reasons for limiting rights are not acceptable, for example on the basis of age, gender or race.

Even when integrity, dignity and equality for individuals is not explicit (as it is in the Constitution of the United States), these principles are the basis for many national constitutions. Influenced by two great 'Declarations of Rights' in the eighteenth century (in the USA in 1776 and in France, following the Revolution in 1789), national constitutions of the nineteenth and twentieth centuries (e.g. the Norwegian Constitution of 1814) recognized a whole series of human rights, although not all of these rights were given even to all adults. The right to vote was, for instance, not generally accorded to women, nor to all men. Even constitutions of generally progressive countries could have discriminatory articles, like the Norwegian Constitution of 1814, which prohibited the entrance of Jews into the country. (This was changed in 1851.) The societal aspect of these constitutions was the establishment of a political system to regulate the legislative, judiciary and active government of society, creating institutions for general benefit, while limiting the state's power to control the individual.

The more important milestone in human rights development internationally was, ironically, an outcome of the horrific denial of human rights in the death camps of Europe during World War II. The Holocaust, followed by the Charter and Judgement at Nüremberg, lay the foundation for *international* recognition of human rights. Although human rights had been discussed internationally prior to Nüremberg, national governments had been able to claim that actions, even human rights violations, which took place within their borders were essentially domestic or national concerns and beyond the jurisdiction of other states or organizations. After Nüremberg, however, the fact that the German government had committed their atrocities within German boundaries and against their own citizens was not enough to insulate them from international condemnation. The governments and the peoples of nations around the globe supported the recognition of human rights as a global issue.

The UN Charter contained clear provisions for the protection and promotion of human rights (Articles 55 and 56), and the Universal Declaration, a resolution of the General Assembly passed without dissent, was quickly accepted as having the status of law, both as authoritative interpretation of the Charter provisions and, in a relatively short time, as customary law. The Universal Declaration was transformed into two binding treaties on human rights: the Covenant on Civil and Political Rights and the Covenant on Economic, Social and Cultural Rights.

The next step in internationalizing human rights was extending the human rights agenda to include particular groups of people – women, minorities, victims of racial apartheid, refugees and stateless people, among others. Also, in 1950, the movement for regional human rights documents was begun with the adoption of the European Convention on Human Rights and Fundamental Freedoms; today there is an American Convention and an African Charter on Human Rights, capitalizing on regionally-shared legal and philosophical traditions.

The balance between individual rights and duties, between which rights are absolute and which subject to societal limitations is important even in international declarations, conventions and covenants on human rights. After World War II, national constitutions emerged which recognized and proclaimed personal and collective liberties and basic rights for citizens in general, including children. According to Ruiz-Gimenez (1989, p.13): 'This was the case in the 1947 Italian Constitution…in the fundamental Bonn law of 1949…in the preamble to the French Constitution of the 4th Republic (in accordance with the 1958 Constitution), the Constitution of the Portuguese Republic of 1976…and the Spanish Constitution of 1978.' There now exists a universal acceptance of the principles of human rights, as illustrated by the large number of international conventions and covenants and their incorporation into national law. Practice – the implementation of the principles – is a different, far more complex matter.

HUMAN RIGHTS: A BASIS FOR DEMOCRACY

As long as he was alone on his desert island, Robinson Crusoe did not need rights. He had liberty and autonomy, but did not need to exercise the rules of social interaction. He had responsibility only for himself, did not have any reason to listen to or scrutinize opinions of others and had no reason to consider the needs, desires, feelings or rights of any other person – until Friday turned up.

There need be no discussion of rights for an isolated individual on a desert island. Rights are always and only relevant in a social context. Freeman (1992, p.28) puts it strongly: 'Rights are relationships; they are institutionally defined rules specifying what people can do in relation to one another.' In so saying,

Freeman also points out that having rights in itself will not improve conditions or people. Rights are about doing, acting within relationships, and are only as useful as their implementation permits.

The ethical, moral and psychological reasons for establishing human rights are interpreted into legal rights through national law and international conventions. Thereby nations and the international community acknowledge that there are advantages to societies in establishing and implementing human rights. Human rights encompass more than the legal rights adopted in each country. In addition to legal rights, human rights can be based on moral, ethical and 'natural' reasoning. According to this reasoning, not upholding these rights would be wrong in any case, regardless of whether or not these rights have also been translated into law. Although not stated in all national law, individuals should, for instance, be entitled to protection against gross harm, such as starvation and lack of necessary shelter. This applies particularly to children, who can hardly be expected to provide for themselves and to learn to respect and obey the laws of a society which does not provide the barest necessities for survival.

The quality of societies and communities, composed of individuals, must depend on how well the individuals function as members of the group, how the needs of each member and the entire group are met and how the group is bound together by common goals. Ideally, a democratic group will give the individual maximum possibilities for development within a common structure of law, social order and common concerns. To uphold the dignity of the individual in the process of formulating common goals and concerns, each individual should have opportunities to influence the process, and decisions should be made in a democratic way. The result should be that decisions made by the majority would not lead to humiliation or loss of self-esteem for members of the minority.

All cultures have established means of transmitting their values and practices to new generations, through the process of education and socialization. This is a continuing process which changes as both the context and the content of a society's beliefs and behaviour change. During childhood, especially the younger years, adult family members are the most important channel of socialization, but siblings, peers and, later on, schools and organizations with adults other than parents are also important.

From an individual point of view, democracy can be seen as a dynamic set of balances between external rules and internal morality, between empathy and assertiveness, between self and others. From the community point of view there are obvious advantages when the individuals fit into the structure of the group. Yet if the structure is too rigid, there can be little space for creativity, little openness to new ideas for change. Particularly in a rapidly changing world, with modern technology, migration of individuals and groups and new mixtures of cultures and traditions, communities need flexibility and tolerance, a climate willing to consider new initiatives. General acceptance of human rights, with the emphasis on respect for the dignity, integrity and value of each individual, can be the basis for community democracy.

Societies which define themselves as democratic place a particularly high value on political socialization, preparation for the participation which is at the heart of any definition of democracy. A key element of democratic thought is the consent of the governed or the sovereignty of the people. Democracies, at least in theory, thrive on an open expression of new and competing ideas, negotiation and conciliation of conflicting viewpoints, public tolerance of broad and competing political organizations, an informed and attentive public and accountability of officials to the people they have been selected or elected to serve. One strong element in a healthy democratic society is teaching its young members fundamental rights and responsibilities. In a troubled and rapidly changing world this may be more important than ever.

NEEDS, RIGHTS AND DIGNITY

One purpose of acknowledging rights is important: acknowledgment creates a new foundation for self-respect and the respect of and for other people. People with the same rights are worthy of the same respect, which is reciprocal and thus involves responsibility in relation to the other as well as to oneself, to listen to and consider the rights and views of others as well as expressing individual views and rights. There is a close connection between rights and dignity (self-respect, self-esteem) and rights and respect (for as well as from others).

In relation to rights it is necessary to distinguish between basic needs and wishes, desires or wants, to understand which claims are reasonable. With respect for the dignity and integrity of the person, basic needs should be respected. Basic needs indicate which rights are important. Basic needs and human rights reciprocally support each other.

Some languages have different words for basic needs and for wishes, desires and wants. In English, however, 'I need' may be used for a wish or desire, for example 'I need a new car'. The basic need in this example might be survival, if transportation is necessary to get to breadwinning work. But a car, and particularly a new one, may not be the only possible means of transportation. For healthy development it is necessary to satisfy the basic needs at least most of the time and in a minimal way, while a child can develop well without getting everything he or she wants, wishes for or desires.

It may be difficult to distinguish what the basic need actually is at times, for example when a child screams for candy in the store. Solutions to the immediate situation may differ according to the underlying need and to the developmental level of the child. Is the child hungry? (A healthier food may be substituted.) Does the child need attention? (A different kind of attention may be better and a different way of asking for attention may need to be learned.) Is the child angry or seeking revenge for some previous distress? (A better way of communicating anger can be learned if the child is mature enough.)

Abraham Maslow (1954) identified a hierarchy of needs which motivate human behaviour. As described by Papalia and Olds (1981, p.18) in ascending order, these needs are:

1. Physiological: for air, food, drink and rest, to achieve balance within the body.

2. Safety: for security, stability, and freedom from fear, anxiety and chaos, achieved with the help of a structure made up of laws and limits.

3. Belonging and love: for affection and intimacy, to be provided by family, friends and lover.

4. Esteem: for self-respect and the respect of others.

5. Self-actualization: the sense that one is doing what one is individually suited for and capable of, to be 'true to one's own nature'.

These basic needs are, as a whole, specifically human and apply to all humans. Needs are expressed and satisfied in different ways in different cultures, reflecting different values. For example, what types of behaviour gain the respect of parents or peers will differ. But the needs themselves are not subject to value judgements, they are universal, while wishes and desires are not. In the same vein, rights connected with basic needs should be indisputable and universal.

Characteristics of the hierarchy are that the person must fulfil the more basic or elemental needs before moving on to the next level. The person who reaches the highest order of needs (self-actualization) is Maslow's ideal, an ideal reached by very few. This person would display high levels of all the following characteristics: perception of reality; acceptance of self, of others and of nature; spontaneity; problem-solving ability; self-direction, detachment and the desire for privacy; freshness of appreciation and richness of emotional reaction; frequency of peak experiences; identification with other human beings; satisfying and changing relationships with other people; a democratic character structure; creativity; and a sense of values. Even though few people ever reach this level, many healthy people keep moving to more self-fulfiling levels. As an ideal, it is a wish for the coming generations.

Maslow's hierarchy does contain another key factor where rights are concerned: Needs-based rights reflect the fact that human rights must always be in relation to other human beings and cannot (or need not) be stated as rights for an individual living entirely alone. Rights in relation to other people involve responsibilities to others and to society. The connection between rights and responsibilities is inseparable. No right exists without its corresponding responsibility. The way rights are exercised and responsibilities carried out will vary in different cultures, again reflecting different cultural values and traditions. Rights, thus, enhance the possibilities for reaching level four of Maslow's hierarchy: self-respect and the respect of others. This connection also makes it clear that rights are not only for the benefit of the individual. Societies need people who have reached the highest possible level of need-fulfilment. Therefore, rights are also for the benefit of societies.

CHAPTER TWO

The Basis for Rights for Children

WHAT IS A 'CHILD'?

Philosophers, historians and teachers may be referring to different concepts when they speak of a 'child' and 'childhood'. Perhaps what is generally perceived as a 'child' or 'childhood' actually only applies to what in the Western world now is called 'preschool children' and is not a universal concept at all. Just 100 years ago children were looked upon not as future adults but as small or miniature adults. This was one of several possible perceptions of children. Other examples include perceiving children as the parents' insurance for care when they grew old, as contributors to the family economy, as possessions with which parents could do as they pleased. Childish impulses could be severely punished, to get rid of them as quickly as possible. Historically, self-support at a young age was accepted in Europe too. From the time of the Roman Empire, through the Middle Ages and the industrial revolution, up to the end of the nineteenth century, European children of six or eight were full-fledged workers on the farms, in shops, factories and professions. Girls of eight to ten were servants in the households of other families. Boys were apprenticed. The ties to parents, home and family were severed or loosened early. According to Aries (1962) two hundred years ago children seven or eight years of age were considered part of the adult world, which would indicate having 'left childhood' behind.

Many descriptions (Hodne and Sogner 1984; Rudberg 1983; Sigsgaard 1979; Tønnessen 1982) confirm that, two or three centuries ago, the children of the farms and smallholdings and of poor families in the towns were working and doing adult work by age seven or eight, particularly the boys. When Hart (1991) writes that '...children [in the 1700s]...were valued for contributing to family work...' (p.53), it might reflect a value placed on the expected contributions in the future, or it might mean that children were not valued until they could contribute. In either case, to be truly esteemed, children at least should have reached a stage where they are able to earn money working, that is, at least six years old (much like the street-children of our time). Other descriptions, for example of well-off families, paint other kinds of pictures of the prevailing perception of what a child and therefore of what 'childhood' was in those classes. In royal families, for instance, arranged marriages could be agreed upon for children of five to eight (a phenomenon still found, e.g. in India), although these marriages might actually take place years later.

DETERMINATIONS OF 'ADULTHOOD' BY AGE

Legal age limits may be subject to change within one country or may vary from country to country, sometimes for less than obvious reasons. In Norway the age of majority was 21 years until 1960. Lowering it to 18 had to do with a new view on the competence of young people. In the USA voting age was lowered as a result of the 'old enough to fight, old enough to vote' campaign at the time of the Vietnam War. Following the same logic, the voting age is 16 years in Nicaragua, where the right to vote is acquired at the same age as the age of conscription. The age-level set for marriage has changed from 12 to 14 for daughters of the 'best families' 200 years ago, to 18 for both sexes now, after a period of being 16 or 18 for girls, 18, 20 or 21 for boys, varying from country to country. This societally-determined level does not have anything to do with puberty or sexual maturity, as the average age of menarche was actually higher two centuries ago and varies somewhat from country to country now. On the other hand, marriage was then necessary to support a girl and also a means of combining fortunes, properties or families. In our time, at least in many industrialized countries and many cultures, marriage is a question of personal commitment, based on personal feelings.

Within criminal justice a variety of limits in different countries illustrate not only how different these limits may be, but also how obligation to take full responsibility for breaking the law can be a gradual process and not something that changes from one day to the next, for example at the individual's eighteenth birthday (see p.134 on children and criminal justice). Using age to determine gradual steps on the way to 'adulthood' reflects the adult society's views on the need to protect children, but also on perceptions of the young person's ability to take responsibility, for example for criminal behaviour or for voting. Some age limits reflect privileges or entitlements society wants to ensure that every child enjoys, such as basic education. One question that must be considered is the appropriateness of the ages set. At times new knowledge will lead to changes. In the USA the legal age for drinking alcohol was lowered from 21 to 18 years, but raised again when it became clear that the lower age led to an increase in car accident fatalities among young drivers.

Age used to set limits can be questioned. The limit applies to an entire cohort, which may seem unfair to children who mature early or to parents who disagree with the limit, for example when they would permit their child access to information or other material prohibited to that age group by law. Yet the age limit may be necessary for practical reasons. It would, for instance, be quite impossible for a librarian to judge each child's maturity in the question of access to certain books deemed harmful to children of that age. Then the issue can become a moral one: Should the parents teach their child to disregard the rules, or should the child be allowed to criticize yet stay within the limits set? Should age limits be more flexible, with room for personal judgement? Some rules do have space for individual assessment, particularly by parents. In Norway a child may attend a movie which is prohibited to children of his or her age, if accompanied by a parent. In some countries the legal age for marriage can be suspended (to a certain degree) if the underage prospective bride or groom obtains permission from guardians, or in some cases from the local authorities.

Another question is what the message being conveyed to children might be. If the age limits are obviously set too high, the majority of children may feel underestimated and with good reason. Yet an age limit set for the purpose of protecting children cannot be set at the level at which half of the children can manage, but the other half still needs the protection. The liberty to choose or to do something from which one has been protected must be set at a level where the majority of children no longer need the protection. So one issue here is whether the limit has been set on the basis of developmental research rather than being due to an adult desire to retain control.

A question today is whether or not children who must support themselves (as street-children must), or children who have children themselves, or children who are active soldiers at the age of 12 should still be considered children. Are they children, or are they actually adults? The concept of 'childhood' and therefore also the concept of 'child' is not as clearly defined as simple age-levels would indicate. Perhaps 'childhood' is really defined by circumstances or by the level of responsibility the person must assume for himself, not by level of maturity. If the level of maturity determines whether a person is adult or not, many adults (as defined by physical size or age) would probably have to be redefined as children.

Even in our own time the period called 'childhood' has different durations in different cultures or under different conditions. In the Western world the age of majority (the right to vote) is generally 18. But current lists of legal rights defined by age, national and international, indicate that there is no one age at which childhood ends and adulthood begins (see Appendix 1). These lists do not indicate at which age a person is expected to support himself or herself, which in many cases starts at age five or six (for example amongst the street-children in India, Latin America and Asia).

Age is commonly used to determine when a person acquires rights, such as the right to drive a car, to marry or to vote. But age also marks the upper limits for special entitlements and protection and the lower limits for attribution of responsibility. The right to free education is, in many countries, lost at age 16. The right to protection by the child welfare system in some countries lasts until the age of majority, but in others may extend beyond that age. Some age-levels are set with the purpose of protecting the child from pain or too much responsibility, for example the age of sexual consent or the age of criminal responsibility.

The age of sexual consent is commonly 16. In many countries this means that it is a crime for a person older than 16 to have sex with a person under 16. The intent was to protect the younger person. However, legislation may not have kept up with changing morals. Nowadays 13 to 15-year-olds have sex with each other, and some believe this is illegal. Or a 15-year-old may consent to sex with a 16 or 17-year-old. While many may react to the morals involved, these situations may not be the kind of seriously harmful situation the law was aiming at. The question of age difference may be more important than actual age.

THE VALUE OF CHILDREN AND OF CHILDHOOD

Descriptions of attitudes toward children through history do not give a picture as clear as some would have it. Cohen (1990) says: 'The early plight of children has been fairly well documented by historians. From Roman times to the mid-nineteenth century they were treated as something akin to property and had rights which might be characterized as falling somewhere between those of slaves and those of animals. Children were maltreated and abused, shipped off to sea, indentured as servants and often sold or left to die' (p.297). Stone (1977) says: 'Children, first considered to be chattel, were valued for contributing to family work and supporting parents in their old age...young children continued to be ignored and were without individual identity to the extent that they were considered replaceable and interchangeable' (Hart 1991, p.53). Their upbringing was so harsh it produced 'distrustful', 'cruel' adults, prone to 'hostility' and 'incapable of close relationships'. According to Hart (1991): 'Gradually, children came to be considered as a special class, and parents were increasingly expected to maintain, educate and protect them' (p.53). One question that arises is how such 'cruel' adults 'incapable of close relationships' can become nurturing, caring parents, able to maintain, educate and protect children.

Such descriptions illustrate changing perceptions of children. They often refer to the two first writers (Aries and DeMause) who described childhood, important because they were the first to consider childhood historically interesting. According to Aries (1962), childhood as a special conception did not emerge until the 17th century, previous to which the special nature of childhood was ignored and children were treated as miniature adults. DeMause (1974) stated: 'The further back in history one goes, the lower the level of child care, and the more likely children are to be killed, abandoned, beaten, terrorized, and sexually abused.' From this we might deduct that abandonment, sexual abuse, etc., should have disappeared in our enlightened times.

There can be little doubt that the conditions described did apply to a number of children, but how many within the entire child population were treated in these ways is unknown, and the impression may be unnecessarily bleak. Other sources provide different interpretations of conditions for and attitudes toward children. Folklore and traditions in different parts of Scandinavia (Hodne and Sogner 1984) indicate that adults felt that small children must be protected and prepared for the future. Children were wanted and cared for to the best of the parents' abilities. For example, parents might feed a baby dried, smoked meat, coffee, or heavy sour-cream porridge in order to give the baby the best available food, as a warm welcome to life (Rudberg 1983). Even suffocation in the bed of their parents need not be a way of reducing the number of children (Sigsgaard 1979), but a consequence of parental attempts to protect the child from evil spirits, kidnapping or the substitution of their own (perfect) baby with a deformed one (the explanation for having a disabled child).

Such beliefs and practices may have led to undesirable results, but on the basis of such material it could be argued that even several hundred years ago parents tried to care for and nurture their children as well as they could, with some understanding of special vulnerability and special needs in very young children.

The cognitively determined attitudes of adults in relation to how children are to be treated may have changed more than their feelings about children. Yet descriptions of the treatment of children can lead to different interpretations. They can be interpreted to reflect the feelings of parents, but may be quite as much a reflection of what parents thought was 'right'. A parent who lost a child might, on the surface, not grieve, which could be – and often has been – interpreted (e.g. by Aries 1962; Sigsgaard 1979) to indicate that parents who expected to lose many children did not really love them, or might be afraid to get too involved with their small children. But if the Church (as in the 16th and 17th centuries) held that the loss of a child was part of God's larger plan, a show of grief would have been perceived as a lack of trust in or respect for God. Therefore, 'unfeeling' parents were behaving according to societal rules. Similarly, if adults believed that children were born evil, the breaking of a child's wilfulness and punishment of 'evil impulses' might make corporal punishment and other harsh reactions seem necessary. Corporal punishment executed by a parent who really felt that 'this hurts me as much as it hurts you' may have had a different quality (and quantity) than corporal punishment inflicted by a parent believing that fate alone determined the destiny of the children. Such a parent would hit a child as an expression of irritation, but hardly with the purpose of beating 'evil' out of the child.

The harsh, hard labour undertaken by children in the past (e.g. being a shepherd at age seven, a maidservant at age ten) could have reflected a belief that hard work was good for children, would keep them out of mischief, strengthen their characters and prepare them for adult occupation and life. But it could also be a question of stark necessity, ensuring the survival of children and of their families when large segments of the population were living in deep poverty. Little is known about the different impacts which conditions like these may have had on children if such conditions occurred in different emotional contexts. A child sent away from home due to dire necessity probably would feel somewhat differently about it than a child sent away as part of an education or as a punishment or because he or she was being rejected by the parents. A different aspect of this was that children were expected to take on quite a lot of responsibility, but this did not stem from nor lead to rights for the same children.

Parental conceptions of children and childhood may be different from the public conceptions, a distinction which may be worth making. Historically, children had few rights. They were denied the right to determine most of the aspects of their own lives. This was a consequence of the publicly dominant view of children. But varying conceptions of children have probably existed side by side, and exist even today, in different parts of the world and in different situations, in part determined by changing economic and social conditions.

Recently an emphasis on the value of childhood *per se* has been gaining ground, particularly emphasized by Qvortrup (1990, 1993). According to this view children should not be perceived as 'not yets' or 'becomings', in the sense that their value lies in their future as adults, but as 'beings'. Childhood as a social phenomenon will exist regardless of the fact that each child outgrows childhood. Money spent on children is regarded as a necessary investment in the future of society. Education of children, for instance, is an absolute necessity for the continued existence and development of every society. Also, children's work in school is their contribution to this aim and should be included in the GNP. Such a view of childhood also means that statistics should include children as individual members of the group, with a focus on them and not only on the adults they are connected with. This means, for instance, that the number of children each couple has may be interesting, but the number of siblings each child has, seeing the number of children in the family from the child's point of view, is at least equally important. Individual children and children as a social class thus become the subjects of concern and interest.

The next logical step in this trend would be using children as the source of information. While Qvortrup (1996) and others have mentioned this as a possibility, asking children about how they view the world is not yet a common part of scientific procedures, which means that many studies lack important information. Interpretation of the results may therefore also be faulty.

For example, in a Norwegian study on the social network of children, preschool children *were* asked, and this uncovered a network of support in their communities of which the parents were unaware.

RIGHTS FOR CHILDREN

As mentioned above, children have probably always had some moral, ethical and 'natural' rights, based on the idea that human offspring have the right to basic care and the right to learn basic skills necessary for survival in their culture.

The idea of some *formalized* rights for children is not new. Two centuries ago the Czech educationist Comenius and the German theologian Martin Luther both declared – in vain – that schooling should be the right of every child. John Locke discussed the relationship between the rights of parents and the rights of the child. In 1900 the Swedish writer Ellen Key in *Barnets Århundre* (The Century of the Child) even demanded that children should have the right to choose their parents, an idea re-proposed by Ulla Jacobsson in the 1980s (Eide 1988). Going back in history the picture is more varied. Several hundred years ago children could have the same rights as adults in limited areas, for example the English child's right to possess (but not dispose of) property. Children could also have rights that adults did not have, such as the right to go to school or the right to special protection in cases of child abuse or neglect.

Acceptance of the concept of *formalized human rights* for children was made possible by converging historical trends. One trend was the advancement of legislation concerning children, the second the emergence of child development as a social science and the third the evolution of human rights. When these three trends converged, beginning in the 1920s to 1930s and gaining strength particularly after World War II, a unique basis for the emergence of the concept of rights for children was established. Changing public attitudes toward children, as distinguished from parental conceptions of children and childhood, had some importance, although attitudes of today are not entirely different from attitudes which seemed to prevail 200 years ago. Also, the attitudes of long ago can surface again under different circumstances today. Such changes can influence views on whether or not children should have rights and how, when and where children should exercise whatever rights they may have. In spite of possible negative reactions, a large majority of the nations of the world have now ratified the UN Convention, signifying that they subscribe to and will defend the rights of the child.

CHILDREN AND THE LAW

Legal rights for children

The earliest legal rights for minors, such as those in England at least two to three centuries ago, gave 'legitimate' children the right to inherit but not dispose of property (which probably was of little consequence to the majority of children). Common law (for example, in England), determined a range of rights of parents and duties in relation to their offspring. Initially, these rules were not easy to enforce, particularly because the law until the nineteenth century did not have provisions for intervention by a superior authority when parental care fell short of minimal standards. The ninteenth century was to become the period when legislation concerning children was introduced in many countries, very often in connection with child labour and education, but also in acknowledging a public responsibility toward orphans and other destitute children.

Such legislation reflects measures considered necessary and acceptable by the lawmaker. Recognition expressed in law also reflected what the lawmakers believed to be acceptable to the general public, that is, the voters (which until the twentieth century included only the male population, and not even all adult males). When a new concept is adopted by 'the general public', proposals for legislative amendment may ensue. In this way developments of law reflect a changing society, changing morals and values and, in some cases, changing institutions (e.g. marriage) or changing interpretations of law. In a democracy these should be consistent with public opinion or a majority view, in which case legislation may enhance the changes (e.g. the US law against segregation or the Scandinavian laws against spanking children). Legislative amendments, based on consistent principles (e.g. of human rights) can close the gap between reality (which changes) and ideals (which do not change, or at least not as much).

During the nineteenth and the early twentieth centuries, child-connected legislation indicated a new concept of the nature of children: They were considered vulnerable, in need of protection. This concept was in contrast to previous conceptions of children as 'innately evil' maintained by, for example, the Calvinists. The 'vulnerable child' had roots in Rousseau's (1762) emphasis on children as innately good but vulnerable to damage caused by society, and in the idea of John Locke (1632–1704) that children were neither good nor bad but malleable. Both emphasized the impact of environment on children, giving reason for concern about the possible effects on children of their living conditions.

During the nineteenth century positive advances in public health had a major impact on child and infant mortality rates. Long-term measures for children became possible (for example education for all children). Industrialization and urbanization led to changes in conditions for children which in turn called for new legislation. Even very young children worked long hours in factories, mines and mills as cheap labor, taking a toll on children which was unknown when they were 'only' working on the farms. These conditions created an acknowledgment of need for new labour legislation.

The skills of professions more complicated than fishing, hunting and farming, which were often passed on from parent to offspring, also made more education necessary. Compulsory school was, however, established for different reasons. In Denmark–Norway (united until 1814) school was compulsory from 1739: learning to read was considered necessary so the children could learn their catechism. It was also stipulated by law that, from the age of 7 until confirmation at about 14, children should attend school every other day, 20 weeks a year (from October until April), which reduced the number of hours spent at work. Views on the benefits and dangers of child labour were mixed, as demonstrated by the fact that laws prohibiting child labour were not always met with unanimous approval. Indeed arguments against the proposals might be strong and sometimes couched in terms of work as beneficial for the child.

In Denmark in 1873 opponents argued that work is a blessing compared to idleness and that any law prohibiting parents from sending their children to work would interfere with the sacred relationship between parents and children (Sigsgaard 1979). Hard work had long traditions as an important part of the training of young delinquents and vagrant children, for instance from the time when 'Children's Houses for Punishment, Upbringing and Manufacture' were established in Denmark–Norway early in the 17th century. In Denmark in 1873 and in Norway in 1892, 150 years after the introduction of compulsory school education, legislation was adopted which in principle banned employment in factories of children less than 14, except for light work which was allowed for those between 12 and 14.

In England development took a different course. 'The child-labour struggle progressed industry by industry and resulted in an eventual adoption of a pattern of half work, half school' (Rosenheim 1973, p.516). In America, universal prohibition of child labour was combined with the introduction of compulsory education. The professed reason was that education must be a basic requirement for a representative government and a classless society, both principles important in the young country. Education would also keep young people usefully occupied, preventing them from loitering. In addition, young people naturally needed training to work in factories and industries.

Legislation prohibiting child labour was often proposed and accepted by adults whose own children did not have to contribute to the support of their family. Lord Robert Owen is one example. His proposal that all children in England should, like his own, go to school led to legislation on compulsory education and a public school system. But this in turn led to other necessary innovations. Many working parents could not support their families without the income of the children. They therefore objected to compulsory education. So free school meals were introduced to compensate the parents' loss of income. The need for supplementary action changes in time. Free school meals existed in England and in Norway during the beginning of the public school system (in Norway also following World War II), but nowadays it is believed that children are adequately fed at home. But the question may arise again as a consequence of longer school hours and out of concern about young people's increasing use of 'junk' foods, or from a recognition of a situation where fewer and fewer children learn the social aspects of sharing meals with a group at home.

Child protection legislation: who was protected?

In many countries, legislation had the dual aims of protecting children and also of protecting society or steering societal development in the desired direction. In many ways this involved control of individuals, including children. Implementation of law was then reactive to the actions of individuals who were breaking the law. With child welfare and other protection-oriented legislation the function of the law was more pro-active, to prevent crime or to ensure rights and privileges. The aim of implementation was to give substance to the rights of individuals.

The reasons for protecting children could be equivocal, involving on the one hand their vulnerability and on the other their future value as adults (which could be reduced if they were damaged while young). In some cases measures to protect or assist children could equally well be devised to protect society, as were, for example, the early institutions for delinquent or vagrant children. So protection was one desired outcome of legislation and control was the other. Idle children might beg, steal or destroy property. School or work would keep them under adult control and protect society as well.

In the twentieth century campaigns for new legislation developed out of a budding concern for groups of children with special needs: the deaf, blind, errant, orphans and the exploited. Rosenheim (1973) concluded that 'the dominant theme of the "new" law [in the twentieth century] has been protection of weaker groups' (p.518). These children were seen as passive recipients, with the inherent possibility that they could be corrupted or misguided. They needed protection but also strengthening through education. Child protection in these terms encompassed the tasks of both salvation and re-education. These were the dominant, underlying purposes of social legislation for children, particularly until the middle of the century. Together with the older law of parent and child laid down over seven centuries, they even now form the modern legal framework for the definition and implementation of permissible standards of behaviour by and toward children. Gradually views changed, so that the focus on the welfare of the child could override the older law of parent and child, for example, the child abuse reporting laws and laws to terminate parental responsibility in the 1960s in the USA. Rosenheim (1973) also finds that 'There is already evident in our legal system an accommodation to the evolving phases of personal development' and discusses possible future legal reforms, for example lowering the age for assuming certain adult responsibilities and replacing coercive punishment measures with more subtle forms of social control, such as withholding benefits. It is, therefore, clear that modern knowledge of child development had, by 1973, become a factor in considering legal measures concerning children. But Rosenheim did not discuss the possibility of rights for children in general.

CHILD DEVELOPMENT AS A SOCIAL SCIENCE:
A NEW BASIS FOR CHILD RIGHTS

The evolution of child development as a social science started less than one hundred years ago. Recent progress in medicine, such as the discovery of X-rays, the understanding of the effects on health of nutrition, sleep and exercise, and new advances in bacteriology and genetics led to an increased interest in the somatic development of children, blooming after World War I in a plethora of comparative studies. Related to this, in particular in connection with genetics, statistics to handle a large number of variables were developed and were used in the construction of tests. With compulsory schooling came an interest in finding out which children were educable, leading to the development of intelligence testing. Studies of the learning process were carried out to determine how to teach and how learning takes place. These studies were also the result of pressure regarding deviant groups (the feebleminded, deaf and blind children, delinquent or socially maladjusted children), parallel to the concern for these groups in the legal field.

In addition to these research and laboratory advances, there was progress in the clinical field, in child guidance clinics, and also in the treatment of adults, where psychoanalysis led to new formulations of theory on child development. By the 1920s both laboratory science and clinical studies were recognized as methods to accumulate knowledge and improve methods.

An enormous increase of interest in physical development and education followed World War I. During the War general conscription had exposed a great number of men whose physical health or education was so poor that they could not serve. After the War, information about children and child care abounded, also because radios were now common in the households and more people were reading magazines and books as well as newspapers. The great burst of research based on the biological approach to development took place in the 1920s and 1930s, when a number of large scale 'growth studies' were initiated (the Berkeley Growth Study in 1928, the Oakland Growth Study in 1932 and the Fels Research Institute Study in 1929, followed by Arnold Gesell at Yale).

The behaviorist approach to learning theory represented by R. Watson and the work of Jean Piaget, influenced by the mental testing movement in the early 1900s, both appeared in the 1920s. Furthermore, the impact of Sigmund Freud began to be felt in the 1920s and 1930s. The practice of child analysis had started before World War I, while observations of children during World War II had led to new formulations based on the 'natural experiments' of refugee children and children separated from their mothers (Freud and Burlingham 1944; Freud and Dann 1954). This had an impact on theory (Bowlby 1969, 1973), as had other experiences and observations (Erikson 1950).

Given the time lag between research reports and acceptance amongst people in general (and parents in particular, who largely look for what they want to confirm their own approaches [Kohn 1963]), it seems natural that the debates of the 1920 and 1930s should reach fruition in the 1950s, particularly spurred on by World War II and the results of its political child-rearing ideologies. Numerous manuals on child care and child-rearing were published during this period, and television brought a new way of spreading information and spurring discussion. The concepts of the value of childhood and its implications for the adult personality, and of the value of children per se, would necessarily be the basis for accepting the concept that children as human beings have rights, but also have special needs and therefore special rights.

Maslow's hierarchy of needs does not exclude children. Since children have the same basic needs as other human beings, it follows that children should be entitled to the same rights as adults, including the right to dignity and respect. Maslow does not indicate how humans develop from the total dependence of babyhood to responsible adults capable of achieving the higher levels of needs. How, when and in relation to whom does a child develop structures 'made up of laws and limits', 'security, stability and freedom from fear' and self-esteem? What are the forces of and the conditions for development from, for instance, stage two to stage four? The fact that children must develop is not an argument against their having rights, assuming that the needs are universal. The necessity of maturation and learning rather points to other aspects:

1. Children need more assistance than many adults to be able to fulfil needs, exercise their rights and take responsibility according to their capacities.

2. The ways in which the needs/rights of children are satisfied will vary as the child grows.

3. The needs/rights of children will be satisfied in different ways in different cultures.

Maslow's theory is not sufficient to explain the changing patterns of need-fulfilment /satisfaction of rights as children grow.

EQUAL HUMAN BEINGS?

When children are considered the property of parents or when they are only viewed as potential adults, they are not seen as individual human beings with their own very special but equal value as humans. Even when they are considered 'equal', they may still not get the same attention or respect for their dignity and integrity which is accorded to adults. This is made evident in many ways. Hitting a child is legal in most countries, while hitting an adult may lead the offender to prison. Working conditions for adults are secured by law – not so for children. Even in schools, where the children vastly outnumber the adults, there are rarely rules which apply to the working conditions of the pupils.

As a general rule, when children do have legalized rights these are indirect, in the sense that others (most often the parents/guardians) have rights on behalf of the child. Even explicit rights are conditional or controlled by others. For example, children in many countries have the right to education. In many countries the law does not actually give the child the right to go to school, but gives parents the right to send their child to school. If the child has the right to education, the parents have a responsibility to get the child to school. So the right to education does not imply a choice for the child. Restating existing national legislation making the child the subject, not the object, of law would lead to a great improvement in the realization of the rights for children in many countries.

Special rights for children?

The general statements of human rights do not exclude children. But the rights of children were not explicit either, being generally submerged with the rights of adults, particularly the rights of parents and family. Since children are human, the general human rights should also apply to them. The International Convention on the Elimination of All Forms of Racial Discrimination does not point to age as a cause for discrimination. But people are discriminated against because of age, the old as well as the young (Franklin 1988). One view on rights for children has been that they were sufficiently taken care of by other treaties, so that special instruments for children were (or should be) unnecessary. The same thinking should apply to other groups such as women or people of different races. But gender and race discrimination are facts, and have been the force behind the 'Discrimination Convention' and the convention on the rights of women. Group-specific treaties have been seen as necessary and have been adopted to protect the interests of weak or disadvantaged groups of people. Children are discriminated against in society and also within their families: As long as children are not perceived as separate, equally valuable individuals as adults, they are bound to lose whenever a conflict of interest between adults and children occurs.

The idea that children should have their own rights did not gain acceptance as an international concept until after World War I. Yet when specific rights for children were recognized, the transition from the first assertions to international law took only 100 years. Some (Cohen 1990) say that the process only took one generation, starting with the adoption of the Declaration of the Rights of the Child in 1959. There was not, they say, any broad theory of rights for children until the drafting process of the Convention actually began.

Children with special needs – special rights?

The special needs of every child and the problems of distinguishing between temporary and lesser special needs which every child may have and the special-needs child raises the question of whether or not children with special needs actually need special rights. The Convention does give them such rights but does not solve the problem of defining 'the child with special needs'. In our view, if every child has the right to have his or her needs met in an adequate way, special rights should actually be unnecessary. The goal of creating optimal conditions for optimal development for every child should be sufficient. However, since this goal is obviously beyond reach in many societies, the emphasis placed on providing special care, education and conditions for children who need them is necessary and understandable. These rights, if implemented, should prevent the tragic fates of the lame, blind, deaf or mentally retarded children who are hidden away or left to fend for themselves.

CHAPTER THREE

The UN Convention
on the Rights of the Child

PRECURSORS TO THE CONVENTION

The UN Convention on the Rights of the Child emerged after the drafting of a series of important human rights treaties, a large number of declarations on human rights and an even larger number of UN resolutions about human rights. As has been stated, the process of codifying human rights at the international level began with the formulation of general human rights instruments – ones which appeared to presume that the provisions would apply to all human beings. These include, most prominently, the UN resolutions in the Universal Declaration of Human Rights (1949) and the two treaties which were drawn up to create formal legal obligations of the rights set forth in the Declaration – the Covenant on Civil and Political Rights and the Covenant on Economic, Social and Cultural Rights (1966). Although some human rights proponents have held that these instruments adequately protect all human beings, others have argued successfully that particular groups encountered particular problems, and therefore needed special conventions to assure the implementation of their rights. The existence of treaties for particular groups provided further grounds for arguing the need for a special treaty on children's rights.

In addition, of course, there was also the history of special documents or special provisions for children's rights. Among these are those mentioned in the Preamble to the Children's Convention itself: The Geneva Declaration on the Rights of the Child (1924); the UN Declaration on the Rights of the Child (1959); Articles 23 and 24 of the Covenant on Civil and Political Rights (1966); Article 10 of the Covenant on Economic, Social and Cultural Rights (1966); the Declaration on Social and Legal Principles relating to the Protection and Welfare of Children, with Special Reference to Foster Placement and Adoption Nationally and Internationally; the UN Standard Minimum Rules for the Administration of Juvenile Justice; and the Declaration on the Protection of Women and Children in Emergency and Armed Conflict.

All of these agreements and provisions imply the special standing of children as a group especially in need of protection. Furthermore, as with women and minorities, there was an increased awareness of the inappropriateness of a singularly 'paternalistic' approach to groups, and the need to acknowledge the autonomy and dignity of individuals, regardless of race, gender, ethnic origin, religion and age. Children, then, in addition to needing protection, it was argued, were also in need of recognition as human beings fully deserving of rights.

The details of the drafting of the Convention are not particularly important for our current discussion, but are found, clearly marked, as relevant to specific articles and topics under discussion below. The process of developing the final treaty was based originally on a discussion of a fairly brief document offered by the Polish government to the Commission on Human Rights, following the adoption of the UN General Assembly of a resolution proclaiming 1979 as the International Year of the Child.

Through the work of representatives of states, international non-governmental organizations and UN staff, the specific substantive provisions and the means of implementation were debated and adopted over a ten year period. The final treaty includes a Preamble, Part I, with 41 operative articles, and Part II, with 12 additional articles on procedures.

THE RIGHTS OF THE CHILD: MAIN ARTICLES AND ISSUES

The rights elaborated in the Convention are normally discussed in four categories: survival, protection, development and participation. The groupings do not imply that the rights are mutally exclusive; on the contrary, the rights in the Convention, as in most rights contexts, are interrelated and mutually reinforcing. It is difficult to imagine how one might plan the implementation of participation rights in disregard of survival rights or development rights. Also, certain guiding principles, for example, the best interest of the child, are most reasonably understood as applying across categories and throughout the treaty.

Survival rights are easily considered to be a prerequisite of other rights. The Convention addresses survival explicitly in Article 6, paragraph 2, requiring states parties to 'ensure to the maximum extent possible the survival...of the child'. Article 6 also explicitly states the child's 'inherent right to life'. Survival is normally understood to also include basic survival needs such as health (Article 24) and adequate standard of living (Article 27). Clearly, survival could also include most of the protective provisions, since without them the life of the child, and certainly the quality of life, would be endangered. But children are most likely to thrive when societies respect the interrelated nature of their rights; isolating physical survival as a goal constitutes a fundamentally flawed approach.

Development rights stress the importance of fostering and nurturing the many dimensions of the child. The same article that states the right to survival includes the right to development (Article 6). These rights include, among others, the child's right to 'the highest attainable standard of health' and 'to benefit from social insurance' (Article 26), 'to education' (Articles 28 and 29) and 'the enjoyment of one's culture, language and religion' (Article 30). The standard of living required by the convention is defined as one which is adequate for 'physical, mental, spiritual, moral and social development' (Article 27), thus pointing to the many aspects of child development. The concern about development is also reflected in Article 23, which provides for development rights for the mentally or physically disabled child.

Protection rights stem from the convention's core of human dignity. These rights include, among others, 'the right to be protected from economic exploitation' (Article 32), 'from the illicit use of...drugs' (Article 33), 'from sexual exploitation and sexual abuse' (Article 34), from torture (Article 37), from abduction (Article 35) and from denial of due process or other criminal and judicial safeguards (Article 40).

Reviewing the provisions of the Convention focusing solely on participation, one discovers that most of the operative articles shed some light on our endeavour to explicate the full range of possible interpretations of the child's right of participation. As a preliminary caveat, one needs to place in context the very notion of a 'right' for several reasons. First, the treaty acknowledges rights for people other than the child – for example, parents, legal guardians, third parties. Second, children themselves may have competing rights – for example, siblings, children of blended families, children of particular ethnic and racial groups. Third, the objectives of the treaty, for example, the support of the family as the natural and fundamental group in society because that environment is considered most conducive to the growth and well-being of the child, acknowledge group rights and the need for community development. The rights discourse often denies or neglects the importance of the social group when pursuing individual rights. As we look at the constellation of rights which describe the child's participation right, we will also place this right in a context of the relevant groups necessary to genuinely fulfil a right of participation – the family, neighborhood, ethnic, religious, educational, national, racial, and other collective units which are at the core of any meaningful conceptualization of participation.

Are some rights superior to others?

The Convention is comprehensive in the sense that it describes rights for children as indivisible and mutually reinforcing. Representatives from developing countries (e.g. at international meetings at ICDC, Florence) have been amongst those who have claimed that some rights of children are more important than others. The right to survival must, they say, be fulfilled before one can begin talking about development rights or participation rights. In this respect they are using Maslow's levels of needs. While survival is necessary, it is not enough. In this connection it is easy to confuse rights and the initiatives needed to provide for the needs of children. If children are starving or dying from avoidable diseases, it is reasonable to feed or inoculate them first. But that does not mean that other rights should be forgotten or can be neglected. The Executive Board of UNICEF has asked: 'What is the use of bringing up children in the world if we cannot ensure their survival? What is the use of ensuring their survival if the lives they are going to have are not worth living? The 'quality of life' ethic is thus coupled with the 'value of life' ethic.' Recent studies (Chavez and Martinez 1979; Glaser *et al.* 1980; McKay *et al.* 1978; Oates *et al.* 1984; Stoch *et al.* 1982) in industrialized *and* developing countries have indicated that nutritional intervention is a necessary but not sufficient mode of treatment for infants suffering from early malnutrition. Nutritional treatment may restore physical growth but does not bring developmental functions back to normal unless coupled with focused and sustained developmental stimulation. The question has been raised if sensory deprivation may lead to less than optimal digestion of nutrients. In any case it would be a mistake, when initiatives and efforts are being made to preserve life, not to consider at the same time how this should be done to ensure that the children saved will develop optimally. In this connection the means chosen, based on knowledge of the psychological as well as the physiological needs of children can make the difference between a healthy and a not so healthy mental development.

A different aspect of this issue is whether or not rights should be granted to children if these rights cannot be maintained during their lives as adults. To educate and train a youngster for a vocation is in itself important, but the importance is limited if the child cannot get a job later on. This highlights the need to tailor education in such a way that its use is flexible and can be adjusted to a future employment situation of which little is known now.

The conclusion then is that the Convention in principle is – and in practical terms should be – applicable for all children in all countries. The secondary conclusion is that knowledge of the needs of children and child development is indispensable even where the difficult situation of children focuses efforts on the basic physiological needs.

Preamble

The preamble of a treaty sets forth the overall goals and objectives of the document and frequently places the treaty in an international legal context. For example, the preamble to the Children's Convention, like those of most human rights agreements drafted under UN auspices, opens with a reference to the Charter and its provisions to the promotion and protection of fundamental human rights. The preamble, also in accord with UN tradition, then refers to the Universal Declaration of Human Rights which proclaims that everyone is entitled to a full range of rights 'without distinction of any kind, such as race, colour, sex, language, religion, political or other opinion, national or social origin, property, birth or other status'. Clearly 'age' is missing from this list.

The first mention of children in the preamble is a protective one – that 'childhood is entitled to special care and assistance', and this protection is elaborated further in the following subparagraph which identifies the family as the appropriate unit for development and children as special family members. A transition to children as active family members is made by a bridge subparagraph claiming support for a family environment of 'happiness, love and understanding' in order to promote the 'full and harmonious development' of the child's personality. The child is then presented in active language as one who 'should be fully prepared to live an individual life in society'. Here participation is clearly implied though not yet formally stated; it would be difficult to imagine how a child could be prepared for an 'individual life' if he or she had not participated in decision-making prior to adulthood.

Important articles

Article 1

Crucial to any effort to develop a framework for discussing a child's participation is some notion of what it means to be a child. The treaty includes language about the age and maturity of the child. The first article of the treaty indirectly acknowledges some of the difficulties with the determination of maturity by age, in setting the definition of the child at 'every human being below the age of 18 years', and then allowing that the age of majority may be set lower. There is no lower limit. Only in the discussion of military service is a lower age actually discussed – here it is set at 15 (Article 38). Clearly, cultural and societal practices vary greatly even within nations, and the first article reveals the thorny problem of trying to establish appropriate behavior, including participation, by the age of the child.

It is interesting to observe here that the term 'child' is, of course, a term used by adults to describe a group younger than themselves. In many cultures, young people entering adolescence reject the term 'child' and, in respect of their wishes, some cultures have a special term which is used to refer to young people about to enter adulthood. The rights and responsibilities of this group are normally seen to be significantly different from younger members of society. For example, a young woman under the age of 18 who has had a baby may be referred to with the term for 'woman' rather than 'girl'. We raise the point to indicate that if the 'child' or 'children' were allowed to participate in the interpretation and implementation of the convention, they might well prefer the use of terms which they find more appropriate to their age/maturity levels.

Article 2

Article 2 is a non-discrimination provision, prohibiting discrimination or punishment on the grounds of 'language, religion, political or other opinion, national, ethnic or social origin, property, disability, birth or other status'. Although the language of the provision is 'protective' and obligates the state not to discriminate, the possibility of a child being included in the identification and determination of such practices is not rejected. The inclusion of the term 'punishment', not normally included in the non-discrimination provision of human rights treaties, highlights a special issue for children. It is not difficult to imagine the beneficial role children could play in development of policies and procedures around punishment, perhaps even leading to replacement of punishment with more positive and effective responses.

Article 3

Here we find the first reference to the 'best interests of the child', a phrase used frequently throughout the treaty. The question that the phrase raises is: 'according to whom?' Well intentioned people with varying values, world views, education, personal experience, to name a few of the variables, may differ on what constitutes the best interests of the child. For our purposes, at some age, even for a very young child, participation by the affected child in establishing what is in his or her best interests is appropriate. Meaningful participation is not the same as control; the child becomes one interested party in the decisions affecting her or his life.

Article 3 also uses the phrase 'protection and care as is necessary for his or her well-being'. Again, the question of determining what promotes the child's well-being is a subjective one and opens an opportunity for participation by the child, including information about options, constraints and likely consequences.

Article 5

Article 5 is the clearest to this point in suggesting the active participation of children in decisions affecting their lives. Parents, extended family members, legal guardians and community members are called upon to provide 'direction and guidance in the exercise by the child of the rights recognized in the present Convention'. The child then is in the forefront in exercising rights, not simply a passive recipient of rights exercised on her or his behalf by an adult. The adult has an important role – direction and guidance – but not determination and control. The provision invites us to a perception of a child who has rights and can act on them, but needs help. The question is: 'how much help?' This question in varying forms was discussed by the drafters, mainly in an effort to clarify the role of family and guarantee that the family would remain 'the natural and fundamental group unit of society'.

The answer to how much help comes, in part, in the most important language in Article 5, and perhaps in the treaty, when considering participation – the guidance must be 'in a manner consistent with the evolving capacities of the child' (see p.47 and Part III for further discussion of evolving capacities of the child). The assumption, then, crucial to the entire interpretation of the treaty, is that the child evolves into an adult and that the level of participation will change as the ability of the child to participate changes. Contrary to some traditional notions of citizenship, for example, a child does not automatically on a particular birthday suddenly become capable of making intelligent decisions about political questions. A commitment to democratic process would entail both education and practice in participatory decision-making prior to the age at which the society has determined formal participation may occur. Article 5 acknowledges that on a full range of social, religious, educational and political issues, children can participate with more or less guidance in accord with their abilities to understand the situation, comprehend the options and consider the consequences of various choices.

Article 12

1. States Parties shall assure to the child who is capable of forming his or her own views the right to express these views freely in all matters affecting the child, the views of the child being given due weight in accordance with the age and maturity of the child.

2. For this purpose, the child shall in particular be provided the opportunity to be heard in any judicial and administrative proceedings affecting the child, either directly, or through a representative or an appropriate body, in a manner consistent with the procedural rules of national law.

The heart of the participatory provisions of the Convention is in Article 12, in combination with Articles 13–16. The interpretation of participation rights implied by the other articles will most reliably rely on these articles.

To begin, the treaty contextualizes participation 'in accordance with the age and maturity of the child'. When a child is capable of forming an opinion, he or she has the right to be informed and to express individual opinions. The child also has the right 'to be heard in any judicial and administrative proceedings affecting the child…', a provision which provides clarification that participation is required in the hearings referred to in Article 9 and elsewhere in the treaty. It supports an inclusionary process of determining 'the best interests of the child' – one that involves participation by the affected child.

Article 13

1. The child shall have the right to freedom of expression; this right shall include freedom to seek, receive and impart information and ideas of all kinds, regardless of frontiers, either orally, in writing or in print, in the form of art, or through any other media of the child's choice.

2. The exercise of this right may be subject to certain restrictions, but these shall only be such as are provided by law and are necessary:

    (a) for respect of the rights or reputations of others; or

    (b) for the protection of national security or of public order (*ordre public*), or of public health or morals.

Basic to democracy is the belief that in order to make intelligent and wise decisions one needs access to relevant information. Article 13 provides the child with the right of access to all forms of information, including a full range of ideas. Also fundamental to democracy is the right to impart information and to express opinions, on the grounds that discussion and free exchange of opinion also encourage better decisions. The secrecy and censorship which are generally considered contrary to the process and results of good democratic decision-making are, in this treaty, rejected as firmly for children as earlier treaties have rejected them for adults.

It is significant that the right defined in Article 13 is global in scope and broad in range, covering art and all media. The justification of restrictions is fairly narrow, although the national security clause is disturbing in its vagueness. It is interesting to note, however, that this set of articles on participation (Articles 12–15) are the only ones that use national security language, and it is limited to this article, not placed in a separate provision of its own as it is in most human rights treaties.

Article 14

1. States Parties shall respect the right of the child to freedom of thought, conscience and religion.

2. States Parties shall respect the rights and duties of the parents and, when applicable, legal guardians, to provide direction to the child in the exercise of his or her right in a manner consistent with the evolving capacities of the child.

3. Freedom to manifest one's religion or beliefs may be subject only to such limitations as are prescribed by law and are necessary to protect public safety, order, health, or morals or the fundamental rights and freedoms of others.

Again, freedom of thought and conscience is a right respected in democracies, normally as an expression of a desire for freedom from state interference.

Religious freedom is a greater variable. Since religious beliefs are often the source of great controversy, and parental, guardian or familial control over the religion of children assumed, this article is an especially strong statement of the participatory rights of the child.

The language of paragraph 2 – 'to provide direction' rather than, for example, to determine – indicates that the child has the right to be involved in decisions about membership in and practice of a particular religion. This right is to be exercised with due consideration to the 'evolving capacities of the child' and, once more, it is not clear what role the child plays in the process and how the capacities are to be determined. Clearly such ambiguity is necessary and desirable given the diversity of cultures as well as the social, cultural, economic, educational and individual differences among the children of the world. Again, the allowable restrictions by the state are narrow but include the public safety (although not the national security) provision.

Article 15

1. States Parties recognize the rights of the child to freedom of association and to freedom of peaceful assembly.

2. No restrictions may be placed on the exercise of these rights other than those imposed in conformity with the law and which are necessary in a democratic society in the interests of national security or public safety, public order (*ordre public*), the protection of public health or morals or the protection of the rights and freedoms of others.

Here we have a very clear statement of a right considered essential to the practice of democracy: to meet with others informally, privately or in public gatherings. It is important to note that there are none of the restrictions of earlier rights, referring to the age of the child, evolving capacities or parental or guardian guidance and direction. The national security exemption appears, repeating the formulations of earlier human rights agreements.

Article 16

1. No child shall be subjected to arbitrary or unlawful interference with his or her privacy, family, home or correspondence, nor to unlawful attacks on his or her honour and reputation.

2. The child has the right to the protection of the law against such interference or attacks.

The treaty in this paragraph strongly states the child's right to privacy and freedom from unlawful interference. The inclusion of family, home and correspondence makes the right especially strong in a domain where parents or guardians have frequently been seen as controlling. The increasing global controversy over whether the law/state power ends at the threshold of the home is stated here in a manner which provides fuel for the full debate. On the one hand, the child's right is one of non-interference. On the other hand, there are no limiting phrases about parental guidance or direction or even about best interests of the child, which implies that others have a strong footing in interpreting how the right would be implemented. The child is the central actor envisioned in the article, participating on her or his own behalf in the determination of what constitutes her or his privacy. Such participation could in itself be seen as a movement of family decision-making from the 'private' secrecy behind the household door to a domain of publicly acknowledged and potentially defended childs' rights.

KEY ISSUES IN THE UNDERSTANDING OF THE CONVENTION

To whom does the Convention apply?

During early sessions of the drafting the representative of the Holy See urged inclusion of the phrase 'before as well as after birth' in the fifth preambular paragraph. Although there was some strong support, other delegations, citing widespread acceptance of the right to choose to have an abortion, argued that the convention should 'remain neutral' on the abortion issue, in part because differences among states on the issue would affect efforts for universal ratification (Detrick 1992, pp.102–3). During the 1989 drafting meetings, the seven member drafting group recommended including a reference that the child 'needs special safeguards and care, including appropriate legal protection, before as well as after birth' (p.110). At the same time the group recommended including a statement in the *travaux* that this preambular paragraph would not prejudice the interpretation of Article 1 or any other article (p.110). [There is no explanation here about how the 'legal' got dropped.]

There is, as shown, no clear lower age limit for the group to which the Convention applies. It applies to all children at least from birth. The upper limit seems clearer: all people 'under age 18'. But there are two exceptions: if the national age limit for majority is lower, this will apply, but it cannot be used to deny children rights under the Convention. Also, if children have rights beyond the age of 18 according to national law, the Convention cannot be used to lower this standard, since national law (Art. 41) supercedes the Convention if national law is the stronger.

Inculcation and indoctrination

Bringing up children to be good citizens as well as good people means that they must learn certain views and values. One question then is who and by which methods such values should be transmitted. The state's concern is to have good citizens. In countries with compulsory public education systems, all children can be the subjects of constant exposure to official values and opinions, from a tender age (usually five, six or seven) and for eight to ten years. There can be little doubt that anyone who seriously wanted to brainwash a population would start when the children are young and impressionable. The schools would be the preferred arena, particularly because the state has a responsibility for the schools and what is taught there – it generally does not have responsibility, nor can it control, what the children are taught at home. Most states respect the authority of parents as paramount to other responsible bodies, some to such a degree that the parental right to authority over their children supercedes public responsibility (except in cases of abuse or grave neglect on the part of the parents). The parents have, for instance, the right to reject education in a public school system in many countries.

While the Convention on the Rights of the Child does not control parents, the principles may represent a challenge to parents. Some would say that parents in countries that are states parties at least have a moral if not legal obligation to bring up their children to function in a democracy. Whether they seek to do so or not, parents cannot help transmitting values to their children (see 'Culture and parental style').

The schools are second only to the family in their contact with and responsibilities for the upbringing and education of children. With the Convention, the question of whether or not children should have the privilege of education because they are small has been resolved. Also, basic tenets for education have been established. When the child is equally worthy of respect for dignity and integrity as any other human being, the consequence must be that teachers and the school as a system must act accordingly. Humiliating a child (for instance by corporal punishment or by shaming) would not be acceptable. Also, within the schools, several of the child's self-expression and participation rights are at stake, particularly the right to free expression, the right to free access to information, freedom of religion (in many, but not all countries), freedom of association and, of course, the right to an education. None of these rights are simple and straightforward in a school setting, partly because a class is composed of many students, with a wide range of capacities, skills and interests, and in many cases with different socio-economic, cultural and ethnic backgrounds. This is, however, precisely why the classroom is (or should be) such a good workshop for learning tolerance and understanding and the rules of democracy. (The issues involved for the individual student will be discussed on p. 109.) In view of a democracy's goal of bringing up good citizens with democratic values, the development of a capacity for critical and creative thinking *should* be a basic concern. Respect for the dignity and integrity of the child rules out indoctrination. In indoctrination only one point of view is presented, reasons are not given, arguments against it are not accepted, even questions are discouraged, thus purposely limiting the child's possibility for independent judgement and thinking.

Inculcation of or insisting on democratic values can be questioned as being indoctrination, but could only be so if done in an undemocratic way, if questions and reasoning were not permitted. In most countries indoctrination is frowned upon, so it might be tempting to propose that the public school system should be value-free and avoid all kinds of transmission of values. This, however, is impossible. Teachers cannot avoid values. Even in selecting which subjects are to be studied, the schools are transmitting values. When they impress upon their students the importance of working hard, of striving to learn, they are teaching values. When they teach conflict resolution or demand that the students respect each other, the students are learning values. The choice of reading materials by the teacher can transmit values. Even subjects taught in school which are relatively value-free, such as maths and physics, are not totally sterile. And there are methods of teaching which promote creative and critical thinking, even in subjects that are more open to value judgements. Critical thinking is promoted when the students are encouraged to ask questions, are provided with a wide range of information, may pursue interests, and when their questions are respected and answered honestly.

Respect for the personhood of the students should lead teachers to take even very young students' challenges seriously and to be prepared to give reasons for their own points of view. They should also be prepared to present other points of view, to tell students that not everybody agrees with what they are saying, and to encourage students to form their own opinions.

Obviously, some ground rules are necessary. Encouraging students to ask questions does not mean that they can all do it all the time, anytime, or at the same time. They will not respect the rights of others unless they learn how. Students must learn to listen and cooperate, out of respect for the teacher (not necessarily as an authority, but as a source of information and a collaborator/helper) and for the sake of transmission of knowledge.

Rights and responsibilities

One of the arguments against accepting rights for children is that they cannot take the responsibilities that go with rights. This argument is rarely, if ever, heard in relation to the rights of adults. There can be no doubt that rights and responsibilities are connected, even when the responsibilities are not explicitly stated. Children should not be excepted. On the contrary, learning to take responsibility is imperative to the individual child as well as to the group to which the child belongs. The question then becomes one of how much responsibility children can or should take. Knowledge about what can be expected as the child matures is important, so the problem is often one of suiting the demands to the child. In many instances even a small child can understand the responsibility that goes with a right. If a five-year-old has the right to attend the movies, he or she will understand that behaviour suited to the situation is the attending responsibility. If need be, what is expected must be explained, and also the consequences of non-appropriate behavior. In other cases, taking part of the responsibility may be appropriate. Giving the child or young person some leeway, for instance like a 'learner's licence' for driving, can make taking responsibility a step-wise process of learning.

A different way of looking at the connection between rights and responsibilities comes from the fact that children may have rights, but these will be meaningless if they are impossible to exercise. There must be a responsibility for ensuring that rights can be exercised and, when children are concerned, this responsibility usually will rest with adults. Adults (parents or other adults or the state) must carry the responsibility for ensuring child survival, for protection of the child and for providing favorable conditions for development. Similarly, participation and self-expression rights impose responsibilities on adults to provide adequate information for choices and consent and opportunities for sharing and gradually taking over decision-making.

Dignity and integrity: two examples

The principle of respecting the dignity and integrity of the child as equal to that accorded to adults has many repercussions in the family, in school and in the courts. The following examples will illustrate how this respect can influence adult behaviour toward the child.

The child and personal privacy

ARTICLE 16

1. No child shall be subjected to arbitrary or unlawful interference with his or her privacy, family, home or correspondence, nor to unlawful attacks on his or her honour and reputation.

2. The child has the right to the protection of the law against such interference or attacks.

Initially the provision stating a right of non-interference was included with the article on freedom of thought and expression, freedoms associated with participation. At that time the article also included a provision protecting the child from incarceration for the exercise of these rights. The debate over the privacy provision covered three central concerns. First, some representatives wanted privacy included in a separate article of the treaty. The working group adopted this idea, reflected in Article 16. The language follows that of the Covenant on Civil and Political Rights. Second, some delegates expressed concern that the provision should be conditioned on 'evolving capacity'. They continued to press for a separate provision on this topic. Third, some expressed concern that the provision might impair the relationship between a child and the family, creating rights for the child which could conflict with that parents. The *travaux* provides no definitive guidelines for interpreting this article, although elsewhere there is language which generally implies that activity within the family is not normally to be viewed as the subject of the treaty.

Privacy is a concept with different meanings, legally and psychologically. 'Privacy' may refer to protection of access to a person's personal space (e.g. one's own room or other space perceived as being under the person's control), protection of access to information about oneself (e.g. a diary, a medical journal) and protection against bodily intrusion (which might include thoughts and feelings, the psychological aspects of self). In any case, privacy has its roots in respect for the dignity and integrity of the person. The way in which privacy is defined and exercised will vary according to culture and situation.

Some might feel that privacy is not a right of small children, which raises the question of when a growing person can expect to have his or her privacy respected. In our opinion it would be better to assume that even the smallest child has the right to respect and therefore privacy rights. In many cultures living conditions are such that the issue of space privacy is hardly relevant to any member of the household. In some ways one can wonder whether the need for privacy is a modern, perhaps a Victorian, concern. In Viking households, parents, children and servants all slept not only in the same room but at least two or three people in each bed. In some African villages and some sections of Western urban culture even now, the whole family shares living and sleeping quarters. This should not be used as an indicator of the quality of life, but indicates that norms differ. Perhaps the issue of space privacy is a Western idea. Similarly, in some cultures the idea of information privacy is not relevant (e.g. where letters, diaries or even medical records do not exist). On the other hand, the principle of non-intrusion is still valid. The possibility of bodily intrusion is probably universal and shows up most clearly in physical and sexual abuse.

The ground rule here should be that the privacy of the child must be respected as highly as the privacy of adults. This might apply for instance over issues of private space (for possessions as well as for the individuals themselves), correspondence and communication. But the issue is not as simple as this. There are exceptions based on the child's maturity, for example that while parents should not read their children's mail, if the child has not yet learned to read it is easy to assume that permission to do so has been given, even when not stated.

More important issues come up as the child grows, such as the question of privacy regarding body. In some respects this is a cultural issue. The norms of the group regarding dress or undress in different situations, whether or not nakedness is a matter of modesty, how and where functions of cleanliness are carried out may clearly differ from culture to culture. Even in the sexual area, where modesty is more universal, the sexual play of children will be regulated according to cultural norms. The sexual experimentation of adolescents is generally carried out in less public places, while adults normally lay claim to privacy regarding sexual activity.

But what if a parent is seriously concerned about the behaviour of a teenager, afraid that the youngster is having irresponsible sex or is trying drugs? Should the parent then investigate the young person's room or diary for clues? Should the issue be discussed first, warning the young person of a possible investigation? The concern of a parent can be irritating, but in general, underneath the surface, the young person very often appreciates and understands the feelings of the adult.

Any presumption that parents have the right to access the private world of their children without permission (or perhaps, even worse, without the child's knowledge) is to deny the child a separate identity. Doing so is to violate the child's trust. (Exceptions must naturally be made when the issue is one of immediate danger to the child or others, exceptions which would also be permissible where adults are concerned.) The issue of a child's right to access to information and treatment in medical contexts, with or without parental knowledge and/or consent, will be discussed below.

Corporal punishment

The Convention, in Article 19, provides that states parties shall take measures to protect the child. Many would contend that corporal punishment clearly falls under these descriptors. The main purpose for including this article was the prevention and prohibition of sexual and other severe forms of abuse. The clearest direct reference to corporal punishment is found in Article 28 and requires that school discipline 'is administered in a manner consistent with the child's human dignity and in conformity with the present Convention'. In order to interpret the concluding phrase, one might consult Article 37, which prohibits torture or other cruel, inhuman or degrading treatment or punishment. At some level, corporal punishment violates the most fundamental foundation of the treaty: the recognition of the essential dignity and integrity of the child.

ARTICLE 19

1. States Parties shall take all appropriate legislative, administrative, social and educational measures to protect the child from all forms of physical or mental violence, injury or abuse, neglect or negligent treatment, maltreatment or exploitation, including sexual abuse, while in the care of parent(s), legal guardian(s) or any other person who has the care of the child.

Corporal punishment can be viewed as a special issue of intrusion of bodily privacy. However, it represents more than a privacy issue and is such a common practice worldwide that it warrants a separate discussion.

Six countries (Sweden, Finland, Norway, Austria, Denmark and Cyprus) have adopted national legislation prohibiting the use of corporal punishment of children. This prohibition includes parents, who in these countries no longer have a legal right to smack, slap, pinch or whip their children, even for purposes of chastisement. When this legislation was in the process of being adopted in Norway, children would call the Ombudsman for Children to verify that physical punishment was actually becoming illegal. Children then spread the word, to adults as well as to other children. There were also generally relieved to know that an 'ordinary' slap would not lead the parent to prison. It is reasonable to believe that many children would not have spoken out if it meant sending a parent to prison or even to court. (For information about the Norwegian Ombudsman for Children, see Flekkøy 1989, 1991, 1993.)

In other countries proposals for such legislation are under way, while in yet other countries cultural or religious traditions are so strong that legislation of this content would be hard to imagine. Yet the Convention is quite clear: children need special safeguards and care and have the right to recognition of their physical and personal integrity. States parties generally accept that child abuse cannot be accepted, but the wider recognition that children have at least the same need and right to be protected against humiliation and physical pain as adults is not so common. Indeed, many countries prohibit the infliction of physical pain to any adult member of society by any other adult member, yet allow parents to hurt their children 'within reasonable limits' or within the traditional rituals (e.g. genital mutilation) of their culture. In some countries the use of physical punishment is actually encouraged.

The Convention challenges all deliberate hurting and humiliation of children, regardless of sex, age, race and culture. This does not mean that all kinds of use of physical power or all infliction of pain are equally offensive. There are situations where physical force or infliction of pain is necessary, for example to save a child's life. But these situations do not involve unnecessary humiliation or lack of respect for the child's integrity.

The Convention challenge is not only based on the principle of the rights of the child but on abundant research indicating that physical punishment is at best useless, at worst harmful. Not all types of physical punishment are equally harmful. The light slap on the hand is often neither very painful nor physically harmful. The harmful effect is probably more in the message that slapping is permissible. As a child-rearing method, for example in trying to stop the small child from touching something, the child learns this at least as fast without the slap, with a firm 'no' from the adult. This type of adult response is also more likely to be generalized, to apply in situations other than the 'do not touch' one.

The other common type of physical reaction is the brief loss of emotional control which leads to the brief loss of physical control. The parent, exasperated beyond endurance, 'explodes' and strikes the child. Any such event is bound to be frightening to the child, but if the occurrence is rare it is probably not permanently harmful. Particularly when explanations are given and forgiveness asked, the child will come to terms with episodes like this, perhaps because there is a certain degree of recognition by the child: He or she also may 'explode' and lose control at times. In cultures where hitting a child is common, this might be the type of corporal reaction most often used. The really physically harmful effect of corporal reaction occurs when the parent does not regain control quickly. Then the distance between loss of control and actual physical abuse is very short.

Other types of reactions to children may be equally or even more harmful than an occasional smack. Shutting children up in dark closets, screaming at them constantly without cause or explanation, belittling or shaming them, or constantly exposing them to lack of attention or concern are typical examples. These behaviours, judged to be possibly detrimental to the emotional/psycho-logical development of children, are also covered by the Norwegian law.

In Egypt, according to Wikan (1985, p.51), hitting is used to correct behaviour but never to humiliate or demean the child's character. It seems reasonable that the negative effect on children is less when the message is: I love you, but I dislike what you are doing. It may be easier to accept and also easier for the child to understand. The Egyptian parents must take the blame for the child's misbehaviour, and there is always some adult ready to comfort the child. Being struck does not therefore mean rejection or humiliation of the child, but of the unacceptable act or behavior. (This still does not mean that hitting is acceptable, although the consequences may differ according to cultural context.)

A more humiliating kind of physical punishment happens when the adult, because of physical superiority, uses that superiority to chastise the child. Punishment is then carried out under emotional and physical control, in 'cold blood', with the explicit purpose of hurting and humiliating the child. There is hardly ever a cause-and-effect relationship behind the behaviour leading to the punishment and the punishment itself. Therefore the experience is not only painful but very difficult to understand for the child. The only clear message is that it is OK to beat another person, particularly one smaller than yourself. This may be why children who are exposed to this type of punishment often exhibit more aggressive behaviour than other children do, particularly in situations which are not similar to the one(s) in which the child was punished.

Proponents of corporal punishment often refer to the Bible. In the public debate preceding adoption of the legislation in Norway, the Ombudsman for Children asked Norwegian theologians for the original text. According to them, the text said that parents who love their child should chastise and discipline. No mention was made of beating. If this is true, some poetic licence in translation may have provided arguments which are not actually in the original text.

In some countries the law specifies different levels of punishment for different degrees of physical assault between adults. But as long as specific legislation does not exist, the child's protection is weaker, not stronger, than that provided for adults. When specific legislation exists, but does not include total prohibition, different levels of 'reasonable chastisement' may exist, such as 'a safe smacking' as contrasted with a beating with some kind of implement. The latter may be forbidden, the former accepted. In neither case do these legislative levels conform with the principles of the UN Convention. Recognizing this, the Expert Committee is encouraging countries to 'find the most effective way in their societies to break cycles of violence that were often perpetuated from generation to generation under the cover of tradition and custom' (CBC/C/SR.136, para.41).

One of the main worries of parents is often based on a misconception. If corporal punishment is not permissible, they equate this with any kind of disciplining, so that they believe that discipline in any shape or form is prohibited. Naturally, if this were true, parents have good reason to be worried as well as upset. So one important message is that parents should discipline their children, but in other ways. Many parents find a 'cause-and-effect' system helpful. According to this way of thinking, there should be a 'cause-and-effect' relationship between the child's action and the resulting reaction. If the child accidentally breaks a cup, slapping or spanking will not teach the child the effect of breaking something. If something is broken, it can perhaps be mended or a new object must be obtained or you have to do without that object. Taking the child's age into consideration, the reaction might be to point out to the child these consequences.

'The best interest' of the child: a difficult guideline

'The best interest of the child' was a phrase widely accepted during the drafting process. However, before the final version was adopted, controversy arose over the exact wording of the phrase itself – how, when and by whom 'best interest' should be determined – and over the relative importance of the interests of the child as compared to the rights of others. The original Polish draft for the treaty included a provision that 'in all actions concerning children the best interest of the child should be the *paramount* consideration' (emphasis added). The USA proposed a different version, that 'best interest' should only apply to 'all *official* actions concerning children' [emphasis added]. Some delegates objected to the use of 'paramount' since it placed children's interests above that of others, because some situations might involve others with equal claims to consideration. The decision was made to change 'paramount consideration' to 'a primary consideration'. Some suggested that the best interest should be 'the' primary consideration, but the working group decided on the looser article 'a', in Article 3, but in other articles (e.g. Article 21 and Article 18[1]) the principle is referred to as 'the paramount consideration'.

Because this concept, used repeatedly in the Convention, is found in one of the 'umbrella' articles of the Convention, it is a keystone and crucial guideline in the convention. 'The best interest of the child' will be invoked to determine the degree and extent of many other rights and to justify or support actions arising under the Convention. It clearly makes the interest of the child more important than the interests of adults. However: 'The central importance of the best interest principle within the CRC framework does not mean that its interpretation or application is in any way straight-forward or uncontroversial. Paradoxically, the greater the agreement as to its centrality, the greater the diversity of approaches advocated in its application' (Alston and Gilmour-Walsh 1996, p.5).

Some of the problems stem from the indeterminate and open-ended character of the principle. Application will not lead to any particular outcome in any given situation, because the criteria are not clearly defined. Cultural and personal values will influence the content or plan of action based on the principle. Therefore it can be used to justify even quite opposite outcomes. Viewing the principle in the context of the Convention as a whole can to some extent clarify the way the principle should be applied, but even as a whole the Convention does not and cannot provide any definitive statement of how the best interests of a child would best be served in a given situation. The implications will vary over time and from one society with its cultural, social and traditional values and realities to another, and also according to the situation and experiences of the individual child or the group of children concerned. As if these considerations were not enough, several of the words used in Article 3 are also unclear. The limits of the term 'concerning' are difficult to discern and can be interpreted to apply to decisions which have an impact on the individual child (e.g. custody) all the way through the range of decision-making to state policies relating to conditions for children. Since the word 'children' rather than 'child' is used, obviously the intention was to include actions concerning children as a whole, the child population of a society. This is further strengthened by the use of the term 'all' (actions), which indicates that any person acting for a child or for children must consider that child's or those children's 'best interest'. However, one debate in the drafting process, as reflected in the rest of the sentence, might indicate that private persons (e.g. parents) are not included. This conflict was resolved 'by adopting the narrower list of persons which did not refer to parents or guardians but did not accept the confinement of the article to *official* actions... Article 3 is of such a nature that it can have application to private actions without seeking to regulate them' (Alston and Gilmour-Walsh 1996, p.16). The expert committee, having adopted the 'best interest' as the guiding principle, has demonstrated how this can be done, by suggesting, for example, that states parties adopt national legislation prohibiting corporal punishment by parents.

'The best interest' as the guiding principle is not evident from the wording of Article 3, which says that this should be a primary consideration. 'The' primary or paramount consideration appears in other articles and in other international instruments, but generally in contexts with a narrower range of possible situations, such as adoption or custody. As noted by the drafting group, there are situations in which competing interests of 'justice and society at large should be of at least equal, if not greater, importance than the interests of the child [when] an approach which gave paramountcy to the children's best interests could not be justified in all of the situations to which the article might apply' (Alston and Gilmour-Walsh 1996, pp.17–18).

Alston concludes that 'the best interests principle is to be applied by all decision-makers, whether public or private, when acting in any matter concerning children. The weight to be given to the principle may vary according to the circumstances, although at the very least it must be an important or primary consideration in all such matters' (p.18). We might also conclude that when the action proposed is not in 'the best interests of the child' the decision-maker must prove why other actions are preferable and why the 'best interest' action is impossible or unfeasible.

This leads to the consideration of how the best interest action may be determined. If based on knowledge of the effects on children of different ages of possible actions, it would seem to require that the decision be made by child development professionals. This would be much simpler if there existed a general agreement, based on long-term, cross-cultural research, about all cause-and-effect results, which would apply to any individual child. Such global recipes for action do not exist. Also, the individual child, as he or she matures, has the right to have a say in decisions which concern the child. The child's immediate wish or opinion may, however, be self-destructive or may not, in the longer run, serve the child's best interest. So the adult must then bring in a consideration of the child's future. (The issue of self-determinism will be discussed at length in later parts of this book.)

So, while it might seem that 'everybody' has some idea of what 'the best interest of the child' means, there is no clear definition, legal or otherwise. It may well be impossible to produce a clear definition, as has been documented by the numerous attempts that have been made (e.g. Freeman and Veerman 1992). Some of these definitions are legal, some psychological, some social/sociological, some medical. Most of the serious ones take into account the complexity of the issue, and that the definition may very well reflect the professional background and the local conditions with which the writer is concerned. Furthermore, it needs to be emphasized that what is in the child's best interest at one age-level or developmental stage is not necessarily in the child's best interest later (or earlier) in life.

Therefore, the question of what is in the child's best interest changes over time. Decisions must at each point in time be based on what knowledge we have about the child's basic needs and developmental level, in the culture in which he or she lives. This is further complicated by the fact that it is not sufficient to look at what would be best for the child at the present time, but a consideration of what would be better in the long run, with an eye on the potential adult, must very often be included. Even when this is attempted, there are several difficulties. First, it may be very difficult, not to say impossible, to know what this child, as an adult, would consider in his or her best interest, at the present time or in the near or distant future. The principle of 'future consent' is therefore questionable at best. Second, the world is changing so quickly that it may be difficult, not to say impossible, to realistically take the demands of the potential situation upon the potential adult into consideration.

In this, but also in other connections, there may also be conflicts between what the child himself/herself perceives as in his/her best interest and what is so perceived by the adults, who amongst themselves may disagree, sometimes violently. And in spite of an increasing body of knowledge about child development, family dynamics and societal impacts on the family as well as the child, the effects of much of what is done for and to children is more or less guess-work. The likelihood for being right in the choices made may in some instances be very high, but the fact remains that for any individual child there is no control-group. Knowledge is often based on research on and the experiences of groups, but the degree of fit to each individual child will never be 100 per cent certain.

The difficulties of good judgement of 'the best interest of the child' can be complicated further by personal factors, such as the lack of knowledge on the part of the parent, ulterior motives camouflaging the real reasons or subconscious motives of the appraiser.

'The evolving capacities' of the child

Article 5

> States Parties shall respect the responsibilities, rights and duties of parents or, where applicable, the members of the extended family or community as provided for by the local custom, legal guardians or other persons legally responsible for the child, to provide, in a manner consistent with the evolving capacities of the child, appropriate direction and guidance in the exercise by the child of the rights recognized in the present Convention.

In the drafting process concern was expressed that the child not be left without any protection within the family. As one delegate put it: 'Any protection from the state given to the family must be equally balanced with the protection of the child within the family' (Detrick 1992, p.158). The development of the article was meant to address two strong concerns: the respect for the evolving capacity of the child and the acknowledgement of the parents as those with primary responsibility for the child. Article 5 emphasized the former, and Article 18 the latter. The attention to the extended family and the community which were eventually included in the article were at first questioned on the grounds that these concepts might interfere with 'the traditional triangular responsibility for the child' (p.161), a notion that would appear to represent a certain bias towards the modern Western nuclear family rather than the 'traditional' family structure in many cultures.

In the final version, the UN Convention on the Rights of the Child accepts the concept of 'the evolving capacities of the child' as a basic principle. By being accepted in the Convention, international endorsement is given to the principle that it is *reasonable* that children are informed and guided and gradually take over more responsibility in matters concerning them. This means that there cannot be a clear 'cut off' date or age for when rights are acquired. Children have the rights described from birth. This seems to be universally accepted where survival, protection and development rights are concerned, but less so regarding participation rights. The gradual acquisition of the possibilities to *exercise* rights is illustrated by the many lists that exist of the different age-levels in different countries for when children and young people can go to school, marry, vote or join the army (see Appendix 1). Age-levels have also changed in the course of history.

These variations illuminate several key issues:

- Rights for children is not an issue created by the adoption of the UN Convention on the Rights of the Child. They have been of concern in many societies for a very long time. (Some national legislations reflecting rights of children date back at least 600 years.)
- The legal situation for girls and boys differs in many countries.
- The age limits vary from country to country in ways that do not seem to have anything to do with differences between the young people, but rather reflect societal needs (e.g. for soldiers) or cultural traditions.

One conclusion must be that there does not exist a global, recognized body of knowledge upon which universal, reasonable age limits may be established. It may be impossible to present such a body of knowledge, but there is reason to believe that we may have available more such knowledge than we are always willing to acknowledge, because doing so might threaten the rights or practices of adults.

Myths and double standards

Objections to the principle of rights for the child are to no small degree based on myths and double standards. One myth maintains that children do not need rights because adults, particularly parents, have the best interest of the child at heart. Thus the only right needed is the child's right to autonomous parents, who would see to it that every child would grow up healthy and happy (Goldstein, Freud and Solnit 1973). In an age when reports of different kinds of child abuse multiply, reality is obviously disregarded by these opponents. Nor do they face the fact that social conditions, many of which are responsibilities of the state or other authorities, prevent parents from providing for all the needs of their children.

The second myth is based on the belief that childhood is a carefree, happy period for all children, who therefore need no special rights. A look at countries where children are killed on the streets or in armed conflict, where children must fend for themselves from a tender age or where children must bear the brunt of increased poverty (which is the case in, for example, some European countries) or where they are employed as slaves reveals the fictional character of this argument. Even conditions that were considered normal a few years ago have disappeared or changed. Safe spaces for play are no longer readily accessible in many urban areas. Children can no longer walk safely to school. The lives of many children, even in affluent, so-called 'safe neighborhoods', are threatened daily, by traffic and by crime.

Other arguments reveal a double standard where children (in contrast to adults) are concerned. Strong proponents of equality between children and adults feel that any differences are morally wrong. To highlight their point of view, they suggest, for example, that one should consider giving children the right to vote from birth, pointing to the fact that the age limit drawn in many countries (18 years) is arbitrary. What is the difference, they say, between 17 years, 364 days, and 18 years? And can it be denied that many young people 16 and younger are politically aware and capable of making informed political choices? They will also say that if rationality and competence are conditions for voting, many adults should be excluded too. Others argue that children are more competent, more capable of self-determination, than they have been given credit for. Both these groups would argue that children should be allowed – or encouraged – to exercise their rights from birth, and that age-levels now set should be lowered or even removed. Given the right to vote, children with the right to choose whether to exercise this right or not would, it is argued, vote when they felt this to be appropriate.

In particular in connection with the child's right to partake in decision-making, questions are raised concerning whether or not the child has the competence for making decisions, at which developmental stage the child has adequate maturity to make which types of decisions. This question is often connected with the idea that there is a need to protect children from too much responsibility, from decisions that are too difficult or from the consequences of unwise decisions. This idea is only legitimate when it is not used as a rationalization, when there is a real need for protection or consideration of the child and what is in his or her best interest.

Incompetence cannot fairly be a good reason for denying rights, for children any more than for adults. If this were done, many adults would also be excluded. But in the present situation there is discrimination against children, who seem to be obliged to prove competence, while adults can only be denied rights if they are proven incompetent. This should also be the principle for children.

One advantage of this would be that instead of having the child prove competence, the adult would have to prove the child's incompetence in order to deny the child the exercise of the right in question. Also, it might encourage children to develop competence. Therefore, a closer look at the actual competence of children is needed, regarding their ability to acquire and use information, make choices, develop and state opinions and participate in decision-making on different levels.

Some adults feel that the rights to have an opinion or some responsibility in decision-making can only be gradually gained by – or accorded to – children. Some adults admit openly that they dread relinquishing their own authority. Others feel that it is better for children if they do not have the rights of adults, with the responsibilities and culpabilities involved, saying, for instance, that children lack the autonomy necessary to engage in adverserial exchange, to protect their own interests and even to know what their own interests are. Such requirements do not apply to adults. These objections seem to be based on a conception that the rights-bearing person must be capable of exercising choice for personal ends and protect personal freedom from the pressure and power of others, which again presupposes a community willing to recognize and enforce individual rights. Where children are concerned, the younger they are, the less able they may be to live up to these concepts. Yet it would be a mistake to object to their having rights for this reason, because these limitations can be overcome, partly by letting children act as far as they are able and partly by having adults (parents or others or institutions, e.g. an Ombudsman) act as representatives of the interests of the child.

Many of the issues raised occur when there seems to be a conflict between different sets of children's rights or between the rights of children and the rights of adults. Some problems concern interpretations of the 'adult' rights when these also apply to children, particularly because children change as they grow. Children of age 5, 10, 15 or 18 are not one homogeneous group. The reference to 'evolving capacities' indicates that the child is not always right and that children cannot be left to decide for themselves. A balance has to be struck between children and adults where both parties have equal rights to be heard and participate in the decision-making process. In this way children can be guaranteed to be themselves, and the right for the child to be a child is protected.

When the double standard involves less respect for the child than for the adult, it goes against the principle of equality and therefore must be wrong. Also arguments based on arbitrary or incomplete knowledge of the child's ability to make decisions or to take the consequences of these decisions may lead to incorrect decisions. But true respect for the child also means respecting the special vulnerabilities and strengths and the evolving capacities of the growing child. In the best interest of the child adults need to respect the child's needs for protection and development, not least the time needed to develop the capacities necessary for exercising rights in as mature a way as possible. In this connection it is important to distinguish between *having* rights and *exercising or expressing* rights. It would be discriminatory if we did not admit and take into consideration that a child is different from an adult, less mature, less experienced, the more so the younger the child is. So in the best interest of the child there is a balance between protecting the child from having to take on too much and giving the child the chance to gain experience. In fact, recognition of this also leads to special obligations. If freedoms are abridged because of the child's lack of competence, this must lead to a moral obligation to develop those competencies that were lacking, but are necessary to exercise that freedom. In so doing, the limitation is rendered unnecessary.

In addition to the possibilities for communication problems already mentioned, there are other possible pitfalls, which at times have been used to argue against participation of children. One is that 'they cannot behave themselves', by which is often meant that 'they do not behave as adults'. This reflects more on the adult than it does on the children, who of course have to learn and cannot be expected to behave as small-size adults, particularly in situations designed by adults for adults. Another is that 'they [the children] are too demanding, they think they can take over the whole show!'. This is often said by adults who (a) are afraid of losing some of their own power, and (b) really think that children *want* to take over all decisions, which they do not.

A third consideration is that children may be expected to take on responsibility for solutions, when giving opinions would be enough. As Stephens puts it: 'The expectation that children have special responsibilities to identify, articulate and propose solutions for adult-created environmental problems parallels the notion that it is the Third World poor – in many respects, the victims of international development policies of previous decades – who are responsible for turning the tide of global processes of environmental degradation and for initiating a new area of "sustainable global development"' (Stephens, quoted by Miljeteig 1994, p.11).

Many problems would be easier to handle, perhaps even solved, if the knowledge we do have was made more readily available to parents as well as politicians. But in discussions preceding and following UN adoption of the Convention, developmental psychologists, educators and other professionals have been surprisingly absent, in spite of the key issues of the Convention about which these professionals have special knowledge. Indeed, professionals with expertise on 'the best interest of the child' and the 'evolving capacities of the child' have, by the terms of the Convention, been given an unprecedented recognition in international law (see Limber and Flekkøy 1995).

PART II

Participation Rights
and Rights of Self-Expression

'Participation rights' is one of the four categories UNICEF has used to simplify understanding of the Convention. The other three groups are 'survival rights', 'development rights' and 'protection rights'. Categorizations like this do not allow the rights to be seen separately. The Convention must always be seen as a whole and the rights in relation to each other. We prefer to include 'self-expression rights' as a sub-category of 'participation rights', because this term more precisely describes some participation rights that may be exercised in solitude or without active interaction with other people. Choices are, for instance, decisions that may be made alone, but none the less may enhance the child's autonomy, feelings of mastery and self-esteem. The first decisions a child makes may be simple choices – for example, which pair of mittens to wear – around the age of one-and-a-half or two. But even before that age the child has clearly demonstrated ability to express feelings and influence family decision-making.

CHAPTER FOUR

International Legal Recognition

Two groups of articles in the Convention reflect the child's rights to participate. The first focuses on the forms of participation and the conditions of participation. Articles 12, 13, 14, 15, 31 and 40 give the child the right to participate by expressing views and opinions orally, in writing or through other media. Article 12, considered by many to be the most important 'participation article', demands that the child's opinion be respected and given due weight when decisions that affect his or her life are taken. There is no age limit attached to this requirement.

While several articles refer to the child's right to participate as an individual, Article 15 spells out the child's right to participate as a member of a group. This is important, because in a group the child learns the power of organization and the tactics and procedures of the democratic process. The group may well be the family, but also groups of peers, which enable the child to deal with the adult world more efficiently. Together they can be stronger than they are individually.

Article 31 specifies participation in cultural and artistic activities, and Articles 12 and 40 concern the child's participation in the juridicial system. Other contexts, including the family or the school, are not specifically mentioned. The Convention concerns first and foremost the relationship of child and State. Therefore, it cannot be used to sanction dynamics within the family. The family can be persuaded, but this can actually be done without mentioning the Convention. There are plenty of reasons for a child-rearing which respects the dignity and the integrity of the child, regardless of the Convention. School may be a different matter, because schools may represent the child's first meeting with public authority, which establishes schools and determines curriculum. Actually, the child will learn the first lessons in practicing the right to influence, state opinions and participate in decision-making in the family, whether the adults want it or not. The difference between the way the Convention would dictate and what parents do may lie mostly in the attitudes of the parents, whether or not they respond with respect for the child's dignity and integrity.

The Convention does place limitations on the child's right to voice opinions. The decision should be in the best interest of the child and it should not be inconsistent with procedural rules or enfringe on other rights or contradict national order. This means that expression of participation rights must be learned and that the evolving capacities of the child, combined with the evolving capacities and the need to protect the child against hazardous decisions or decisions which may lead to consequences the child cannot handle, must determine how the child can express opinions and share in the decision-making process.

The other group or participation rights focus on the requirements of participation. Some paragraphs within one group overlap with the content of the other group, so, as always, it is necessary to see the Convention as a whole and not consider articles isolated from the context. The responsibilities of parents are not only concerned with bringing the child up in a way appropriate with his or her evolving capacities. Parents are also responsible for appropriate direction and guidance, and the state is responsible for necessary assistance to the parents. Appropriate information is a requirement for formulating a rational and sound opinion. But what happens when the state, perhaps represented by the schools, and the parents disagree on what *is* 'appropriate' information? Often they will agree. Certain information will obviously be important for the development of the child, and some will by consensus be injurious to the child's well-being. But there may be grey zones, and the school may then provide information that the parents would rather prefer that the child have later or not at all.

To summarize, in the UN Convention self-expression and participation rights mainly appear in Articles 12–16. They include the rights to information (Article 13), the freedom to express opinions and to have his or her opinions taken into account in any matter or procedure affecting the child (Articles 12 and 13) This means that the child *may* have a say in matters concerning his or her life and shall be provided the opportunity to be heard, particularly in any judicial or administrative procedure affecting the child. (However, having the opportunity to be heard does *not* preclude the option of choosing not to give an opinion.) The child shall have right to freedom of association (Article 15) and of thought, conscience and religion (Article 14), subject to appropriate parental guidance and national law, 'in a manner consistent with the evolving capacities of the child' (Article 14.2). In these ways, the Convention gives the child the right, with increasing maturity, to increasingly participate in activities of society and take a part in decision-making, in school and in the widening circle of local community, and the states parties have a commitment to provide the necessary conditions for exercising these rights.

CHAPTER FIVE

Foundations for Participation and Self-Expression

POLITICAL RATIONALE FOR PARTICIPATION RIGHTS

Political theorists continue to debate the possibility, benefits and efficacy of political participation. Their ideas shed light on our understanding of why democratic societies benefit from enhanced participation by all its members.

Pateman argues that participatory democracy can exist on a large scale and that representation is only one necessary but not sufficient requirement for democratic society. Relevant to our discussion is her claim that participatory society is necessary in order to provide people with the social training needed for representative government to be democratic. Participation beyond government would mean that ordinary people are 'better able to assess the performance of representatives at the national level, better equipped to take decisions of national scope when the opportunity arose to do so, and better able to weigh up the impact of decisions taken by national representatives on his [sic] own life and immediate surroundings' (Pateman 1970, p.110).

In Pateman's view participation becomes part of the work of the world. In addition, her evidence on the effects of the democratization of industry, which she sees as the most important sphere in educating citizens in political participation, shows that workers can 'exercise almost complete control over their jobs and participate in a wide range of decision-making, without any loss in productive efficiency' (p.62). In many cases productivity actually increases. Pateman does not directly address the situation of children and youth, but her arguments very directly support the notion that the engagement of young people in the democratic process in all areas of life benefits not only the individuals involved but the general society as well.

Nagel's work also contributes to our understanding of the values of participation for the society as well as the individual. He believes that there are many effects to participation, but among those most relevant to our work are some of what he refers to as developmental and intrinsic effects. 'Participation has developmental, or educative effects, to the extent that the process of participation itself changes participants by developing in them new values, attitudes, skills, knowledge, and beliefs' (Nagel 1987, p.13). People may learn about the system and how it works, improving their skills and their decision-making ability. As they work with others, they learn about difference and how to work together and broaden their view beyond their own narrow self-interest. They may begin to 'appreciate the need to extend rights to everyone' (p.13). And the system is also improved if the participation elicits greater commitment to the system. (p.14) Participation can lead to a better appreciation of the arguments and a greater level of compliance.

The process of participation itself may lead to intrinsic benefits, according to Nagel. Among the most important 'are an enhanced sense of one's own individual worth and an intensified identification with one's community' (p.14) And Jack Lively argues that the political activity is crucial to democracy. 'This idea of citizenship as a stamp denoting communal acknowledgement of individual worth has historically provided probably the strongest emotional thrust towards democracy' (Lively as quoted by Nagel 1987, p.15).

Thus, participation theorists lay a firm groundwork for our arguments that children and youths need opportunities to participate both for their own developmental benefit and for the benefit of the democratic societies of which they are a part. These benefits are not limited to their role as 'future adults' but also as current potentially contributing members of their families, schools, religious organizations, clubs and communities.

SOCIAL CONSEQUENCES OF PARTICIPATION

Learning democracy for a changing world

A Danish philosopher once jested that 'prediction is difficult, particularly about the future'. The world is changing faster than ever. It is nearly impossible to predict what society will look like and which skills today's children will need 15 to 20 years from now. Even the computer skills children learn at age 10 are very likely to be antiquated when they reach 15 or 20. Communities and populations that function according to traditions established during the past centuries will be affected by modern technology. As they grow up, the children will need skills their parents never heard of. Already children need to acquire skills and competencies which will prepare them for a variety of possible futures. Communication skills and social skills will be important in any kind of future community. But to be able to adjust to rapid changes and to function in democratic societies, future adults will need personality characteristics which include tolerance, creativity, flexibility, persistence, courage, self-confidence and a strong sense of justice and of responsibility. These traits develop gradually and must be nurtured from the early years of childhood.

'Wild children' brought up by animals or in isolation have demonstrated how crucial social interaction is to learning the language, norms and social rules of society. As the child grows, he/she must not only learn the 'external' rules governing social interaction, but these must be internalized. Gradually the rules must also be merged or combined with a sense of morality, so that the individual can make socially acceptable judgements, choices and decisions even when there are no external rules or nobody else is present to oversee the actions of the individual. Social learning has to do with cognition, reasoning and understanding, but also with emotional experiences and maturity. From the early empathy of toddlers the child ideally develops a willingness to forfeit satisfaction of his/her own desires for the benefit of others.

To function in a democracy children must gradually learn to take their share of responsibility for themselves and for the groups to which they belong, based on a feeling of belonging and of identification with the group. They must be able to express opinions and to know when to give in and when to persist. They must be able to make decisions with due consideration of other people. Consideration of others and acceptance of responsibility are not learned from one day to the next. If children are to respect and have tolerance for others, including people of different ages, genders, race, nationalities, traditions and cultures, they must be met with that same kind of respect themselves, for their own dignity and integrity as well as for their differences.

With an increasing participation from children and young people, with the aim of developing democratic conflict and problem resolution, many groups and communities will find that the experiences and special views of children add valuable insight and creative suggestions to the problem-solving process. This has been demonstrated in many local communities that have already brought children into the process and on the national level, for example in Norway through the work of the Ombudsman for Children. The benefit to the children has been, amongst other things, a strengthening of hope for the future, combating young people's depression. The future of the world should benefit if future generations are more able to exercise peaceful and constructive methods for conflict resolution than have the past and present adult generations.

Self-expression, the Convention and the family

The UN Convention is a convention undertaken by states parties. It recognizes and emphasizes the importance of the family and the responsibilities of parents (Articles 3 and 5 and the Preamble) and does not directly regulate family life (see Cohen and Bitensky 1996). The Convention is, however, quite clear that the primary responsibility for the care and raising of children lies with the parents, not the state. Article 18 states: 'Parents or, as the case may be, legal guardians, have the primary responsibility for the upbringing and development of the child.' The role of the state is clearly a helping one: 'States Parties shall render appropriate assistance to parents and legal guardians in the performance of their child-rearing responsibilities.' And Article 27 identifies the parents as the ones primarily responsible for the financial support of the child, while the state is assigned the role of assisting parents.

Throughout the drafting there was never any controversy over this fundamental distribution of power and responsibility. Further support for this interpretation of the basic recognition of the primary role of parents or legal guardians is found in Article 5: 'States Parties shall respect the responsibilities, rights, and duties of parents or, where applicable, the members of the extended family or community...to provide...appropriate direction and guidance in the exercise by the child of the rights recognized in the present Convention.' The discussion of this article by drafters, again, did not challenge the primary role of the family; rather, refinements were offered which identified the community and extended family as having a significant role to play and brought further into the treaty the important language on the evolving capacity of the child. As noted, the importance of the family is seen throughout the treaty. Article 9 requires states parties to 'ensure that the child shall not be separated from his or her parents'. Only under extreme circumstances, where the best interest of the child requires it, may the state separate a child from the parents; the example given is that of neglect and abuse. Even then, the procedure must be subject to judicial review, and regular contact between child and parents is required, unless contrary to the child's best interest. A further reflection of the heavy weight placed on the primary importance of the family is the requirement found in Article 10, which obligates the state to co-operate in family reunification efforts.

The Convention does emphasize responsibilities of parents, such as the responsibility to give the child not only information but also 'direction and guidance in the exercise by the child of the rights recognized in the present Convention' (Article 5) and 'direction...in the exercise of his or her right in a manner consistent with the evolving capacities of the child' (Article 12.2). But the Convention is about individual rights for children and the commitments of the state in relation to each child. Acknowledging the child's right to information and participation may not lead to drastic changes, particularly within families.

The role of the child in making decisions about preserving the family is addressed in several articles. Article 8 states the right generally as 'the right of the child to preserve his or her...family relations'. In addition, the Convention in several articles stresses the need to preserve the family at various times of crisis. In all these instances, the right of the child to participate in defining her or his own level of involvement, considering the context and the capacity of the child, is directly stated or implied. For example, Article 9 addresses the selection of residence when parents are separated and with the placement of the child in abuse and neglect cases. All interested parties are 'to participate in the proceedings and make their views known'. It is difficult to imagine a strong argument which would contend that the child is not 'an interested party'. And if a parent is taken into custody, the child has the right to request information about the parent. Article 10 addresses the issue of family reunification and identifies the child as one person entitled to initiate an application, including a choice to leave any country, including one's own.

Article 20 focuses on the status of children's rights in connection with adoption, foster care and the *kafalah* of Islamic law (see p.130). The language does not require but allows consultation with the child about the 'desirability of continuity in a child's upbringing and to the child's ethnic, religious, cultural, and linguisitic background'. And Article 21 is completely focused on issues related to adoption, including a requirement of informed consent which, depending on her or his abilities, would include the consent of the child. Further concern with family preservation arises in Article 22, dealing with refugee children. The provision requires states to 'assist such a child and to trace the parents or other members of the family of any refugee child'. In the event that a child is deprived of liberty, the child is entitled under Article 37 to have access to her or his family.

The methods used in teaching, training and bringing up children vary from culture to culture and also from generation to generation. Research exists on the effects of some methods. Whether or not the Convention will lead to changes in how parents treat their children remains to be seen, particularly because the Convention does not regulate behaviour or attitudes within the family. Some changes may come anyway, because families are influenced by the society in which they operate and the Convention does prescribe commitments for the state. One commitment is the state's responsibility for providing as adequate conditions as possible for children and families, for example for health care and education. These conditions must also include possibilities for exercising participation rights outside the family circle. Many of the articles of the Convention touch upon participation rights or can be discussed in relation to how they look from the viewpoint of the child. Health issues and other survival rights, education and other development issues can become areas of possible child involvement.

The Convention also affirms respect for traditions and beliefs of parents, as long as they are not harmful to the child. It might also be worth pointing out that the Convention does not control what goes on within the family. The obligation to comply with the Convention lies with the state party, which in turn can and should use measures to improve the conditions of children. Some of these measures will have an effect upon or within the family circle, for example improvements in financial support to families, or legislation prohibiting the use of corporal punishment. In the countries which have adopted the latter legislation, no sanctions are involved. Thus, with the exception of cases of physical abuse, the aim of this legislation is to describe the public attitude towards physical punishment, not to have a means of imprisonment of parents. But the legislation might be conveying a far more important message to children than how to avoid a spanking: the use of physical punishment coercion or violence is not an acceptable way to solve conflicts or control other people.

But while the Convention may prevent the family's interference with the child's possibilities for exercising his or her rights, the treaty as such is concerned with the relationship between the *child* and the state. This may also be seen as an expression of the need to balance protection of the rights of the child and protection and preservation of the family. There is no way the Convention or its monitoring bodies can invade, intrude upon or sanction what parents do to their own children. When parenting needs monitoring, this is undertaken by local groups or services according to national legislation or common law.

One aim of the following discussions is to clarify how children, from the moment of birth, actually have an impact on decision-making in their environment and how the ways in which they can participate change with their evolving capacities. This development could be described without any reference to the UN Convention. However, the Convention has now been accepted by all but a very small number of the nations of the world. Therefore, it sets a new international standard for the participation and self-expression of children. So even though many children would participate regardless of the Convention, it is of interest to investigate how child development and legal standards fit together and how the Convention can be used to help clarify and legitimize movements to improve conditions for children.

The Convention does not propose giving children a total range of decision-making powers, regardless of age and maturity, culture, family situation and society. Age and maturity are reflected in the basic concerns for 'the evolving capacities' and 'the best interest' of the child. The extent of participation – that is, the rights to express opinions, to have these opinions considered, to play some role in decision-making and to make individual decisions – must, in the best interest of the child, be balanced with the rights for protection and development. That is why the issue of exercising participation rights is not as simple as that of survival rights, and will vary with age, culture, etc. Also, adults fear that parents will have to relinquish power over their children. If power implies an autocratic attitude toward children, perhaps some power *should* be given up. But if power means authority, children can be seriously deprived of important learning if parents – while relinquishing an authoritarian role – do not remember that they are authorities. That means that parents should impart the wisdom, experience and insight they have acquired, so children will know that their parents can be trusted to protect and support them, with respect for the child's dignity and integrity.

The family: the smallest democracy

The first, most lasting and most important setting in which development takes place is the family. What constitutes 'a family' varies from culture to culture. In many parts of the world 'the family' has changed a great deal during the past generation. New kinds of families, such as single-parent families or families including step-parents as well as birth-parents, step-siblings and half-siblings, are common now. Growing up in a foster family is common nowadays but may have been even more common in earlier times. (Viking children often grew up in more noble families while medieval parents often let their sons grow up in the family of the guild to which they were apprenticed.) However, even a family group with two members is sufficient to be labelled 'the smallest democracy'.

As in other democratic systems, a democratic family is characterized by mutual respect, sharing, integrity, autonomy and equality in the sense that each member, while not identical, has equal value as a human being. In the adult–child relationship the integrity of each person and their mutual respect may be constant, while the degree of actual autonomy or freedom of action is limited and changes over time, partly because of consideration of the other person, partly due to the developmental stages and capacities of the members. Developing a healthy balance between the consideration of the needs of its members is one of the goals of democratic family functioning. Because the needs of children and adults change over time, this process is constant and ongoing, never completed. It involves sharing responsibility, so that children as they develop can learn to take responsibility, first for themselves, later for other family members, and finally in the world outside the family. To make this possible they must have opportunities to participate in the small democracy of their families and, as they grow, in the democratic decision-making of organizations, institutions and communities.

THE PSYCHOSOCIAL RATIONALE FOR SELF-EXPRESSION RIGHTS

Survival, protection and development rights seem to be universally perceived as obviously reasonable, based on the child's basic needs from birth. How to provide for these rights is an overwhelming problem in many parts of the world, but the principle of having such rights is accepted. In contrast to survival, protection and development rights, participation rights seem more controversial, in part because the ways to exercise or fulfil these rights are not as immediately obvious nor as simple to evaluate as other rights. The main uneasiness concerns the fear that children's rights will conflict with those of parents. Some feel that these Convention articles are less definite than others, which may be due to an awareness of possible conflicts involved between the rights of the child and the rights of adults, particularly parents.

There are always some conflicts involved in having and exercising rights, some of which are raised particularly where children are concerned. A child has rights of self-expression and self-determination. But how far-reaching are these rights? Can a child, when faced with an unpleasant school situation for instance, decide that he or she does not want to go to school? Or decide that he or she does not want a particular medical procedure? What happens if the parent disagrees with the child's choice of friends, church or activity? And what if the rights of one child in a family do not coincide with the rights of a sibling? These examples illustrate several important issues, particularly for children. The child has rights, but like adults there can be reasons for not choosing or being unable to exercise the rights, or situations in which it is impossible to do so. The adult, for instance, has the right to vote but may choose not to do so. The rights of the child must also be seen as a complex, dynamic totality, where rights for self-expression and self-determination must be weighed with or against the rights for protection and development. The 'best interest of the child' and the child's evolving capacities are always the guidelines for choice. This means that the child may not be allowed to make decisions, but it does not mean that he or she loses the right to voice an opinion (if he or she wants to and is able to do so) or the right to be informed about the reasons for a different decision.

Self-expression rights and personality development

The basis for the Convention of the Rights of the Child is the universal human rights principle that every person has the right to be treated with respect for his or her dignity and integrity. This applies to all rights, but is perhaps more necessary to remember where the rights of self-expression and participation are concerned than for simple survival. Perhaps there is a continuum from a minimum of respect needed to provide for the physical needs and rights of the child, through development and protection rights, to the rights of self-expression. It is, in any case, extremely difficult to imagine how a child can continue to express or exercise the rights of self-expression if he or she is not met with adult approval and respect.

In addition to ethical, moral and legal reasons for rights for children, there are psychological reasons as well. Rights add a dimension of respect for the dignity and integrity of the child as a person which may otherwise be lacking, even when the child's basic needs are satisfied.

The Convention thus emphasizes that adult, including parental, attitudes to children should be based on respect for the child as a person. While attitudes can only be changed over time, the Convention can be seen as an instrument to further attitudinal change, from viewing the child as a possession and treating him or her as an object, to seeing the child as an individual. The shift in child-rearing patterns would accordingly be from the authoritarian to the authoritative. It is difficult to imagine how adult oppression, as distinguished from discipline, can be combined with respect for the child. Oppression may lead to the child experiencing humiliation, hopelessness and resignation, with low self-esteem and little faith in his or her own attempts to make decisions or voice opinions. Many children with oppressive parents will have their basic physical needs taken care of but may suffer emotionally and socially.

If the goal of child-rearing is self-reliant, self-controlled, explorative and contented children, the positive effect of an authoritative upbringing for the development of the child was indicated long before the Convention was adopted. Studies of methods of child-rearing (e.g. Baumrind 1971a, 1971b, 1975, 1980) indicate that authoritarian practices, which are more or less oppressive, lead to more discontented, withdrawn and distrustful children, who also show more aggressive behaviour, with fewer skills in democratic group functioning. In contrast, authoritative parents enforce rules and demand high levels of achievement, and are receptive to the child's questions, comments and suggestions. Clear limits and rules, suited to the child's developmental level, seem to give the child a framework within which there are opportunities to learn socially acceptable behaviour.

For school-age children Coopersmith (1967) found that personal charac-teristics of the parents appeared to contribute to their children's level of self-esteem. Parents who fail to define and enforce clear limits of acceptable behaviour are more likely to have children with low self-esteem. Fischer and Lazarson (1984) state that when children develop feelings of inferiority, the process commonly begins with parents who treat their children in a rejecting, distant or autocratic way. Overly permissive parents may actually be distant and indifferent except when trouble arises, at which point they may punish the child for breaking rules that never were clearly established beforehand.

When the child's behavioural possibilities are taken into account, rule-set-ting also contains a strong element of respect. When the demands made are within the child's capacities, success in living up to them leads to feelings of accomplishment, self-esteem and self-confidence. Authoritative child-rearing practices (which are also exercised by adults other than the parents) clearly conform with the rights – not only the needs – of the child. Interestingly, one of the earliest research projects which illuminates the value of participation with adult support concerns school-age children and was carried out by Lewin, Lippitt and White in 1936 (Lippitt 1940). In the 'democratic' group, the boys made the plans for the project as well as the rules for cooperation, in contrast to the authoritarian group (run by the adult) and the 'laissez-faire' group (no leadership, no rules). The democratic group had better results as well as less aggression and the members were also more satisfied by their efforts.

The importance of a 'sense of self'

Being treated with respect for personal dignity and integrity should enhance the child's development of self-esteem, self-confidence and the 'sense of inner competence'. Investigators (Rutter 1979, 1987) have identified the child's 'sense of self' as a key determinant for successful developmental outcomes. It is suggested that children with positive feelings of self-esteem, mastery and control can more easily manage stressful experiences, which in turn leads to more positive reactions from their environment. They show initiative in task accomplishment and relationship formation. Even in stressed families, one good relationship with a parent reduces psychosocial risk. For older children a close, enduring relationship with an external supportive adult may provide a protective function.

A positive self-concept seems to be the starting point of a good cycle even under difficult circumstances, such as deprived environments: the child seeks, establishes and maintains the kinds of supportive relationships and experiences that promote successful outcomes. These successes feed back positively in the self-esteem and sense of mastery of the child, leading to further positive experiences and relationships and more success. The cycle can in this way become self-perpetuating.

CHAPTER SIX

Considerations in the Practical Application of Rights

PARTICIPATION AND PROTECTION

Gaining full use of participation rights is a gradual process, starting at birth (or before) and ending when the person acquires and can exercise all the rights of their population group. Full and free possibilities to exercise these rights may never be entirely attained by all people, which is why human rights monitoring is still necessary.

In view of the Convention, self-expression and participation rights must be seen in relation to the rights to development and protection. Whether or not the child in general needs protection is not a matter for discussion. The discussion starts when the question arises of when, how and in relation to whom the child shall exercise self-expression and participation rights; which decisions the child needs to be protected from; and when and in relation to what kinds of situation the child should be relieved of any obligation to form and express an opinion. In principle children, like adults, enjoy all rights with some (few) exceptions, but they need more protection and more guidance than adults.

Overprotection, protection and underprotection

Based on more detailed knowledge about the real competence of children, it should be possible to protect when necessary, without overprotecting. 'The best interest of the child' and 'the evolving capacities' are the guiding principles. 'Competence' needs clarification. 'Protection' also needs clarification. Some (e.g. Verhellen 1993) feel that children do not need protection, although their rights do. It should not be forgotten, however, that protection of children is not discrimination. *All* people need protection at some time or other, in different situations. Nor is the dependency of children a reason to deny them their rights, both because all humans are dependent upon others at least some of the time and because negotiation of participation, based on respect, can very well be carried out in relation to dependent persons.

The need for protection is recognized in international human rights treaties and also in national laws. Labour laws protect employers and workers in various ways. Traffic rules aim to protect drivers and pedestrians. Health legislation is tailored to protect the health of young and old. Legislation for the protection of children is weaker than that for adults. But there can be no question that children need protection. The question is what kind of protection, by whom and through which means protection should be provided. Perhaps we can think of this as an axis system, with age/maturity along one axis. Complexity of problems to be confronted would be on the other axis, from simple expression of needs to simple choices, from everyday situations in the family to decision-making in the community. As age and maturity increase, protection needs where the simple problems are concerned would decrease.

The kinds of decisions also need to be considered. Simple choices in everyday situations need not pose problems but more complicated choices, such as medical alternatives, are difficult, not only due to the complexity involved but also because children generally have less experience with these types of circumstances and their consequences. The types of choice which have been the subject for laboratory research have often involved exactly these kinds of choices, with middle-class children from industrialized countries. In spite of the obvious need for more research, the research thus far seems to indicate that by age 15 there is no reason on the basis of competence to deny minors rights of self-determination, at least in areas of treatment decisions. (Grisso and Vierling 1978; Weithorn 1980; referred to by Melton (1983, pp. 14–16) and Weithorn (1983) and Lewis (1983). According to Weithorn (1980), nine-year-olds would tend to reach the same conclusions as the teenagers in the laboratory situation. We do not know, but there may be reason to speculate that even younger children, if the situation is well-known and the alternatives made clear in language understood by the child, could be more competent than expected in the question of consent or making such choices, at least in a laboratory setting.

The protection children need in order to exercise their rights often involves a discussion of where and in what context children can give opinions and play a part in the decision-making process. When discussing where children should be able to exercise their rights, the focus is often on arenas. The family is one such arena (although not regulated by the Convention). Schools and local communities are other arenas. In many connections the question is raised of how to create arenas for children to exercise their participation rights, that is get experience in political decision-making. While this is a valid issue, we must first recognize and accept the arenas that are already there and recognize and honour children as players already on the field. These arenas include the family but also include nursery-schools, classrooms and other everyday life situations where, with little or no change, the participation of children can be enhanced. The most basic change needed is in attitude: When adults in any situation reflect upon the possibilities for child participation, there will be no need to look for or construct arenas. The arenas are already there, if we know how to use them.

Legislation in many countries limits or restricts children's participation in decision-making processes. There may well be a need to take a close look at these laws, to see if they are actually based on concern for the child or whether the interest of the child is used as a smokescreen. Such legislation should not be designed to avoid incompetence per se, but to enhance welfare or minimize harm (Melton, Koocher and Saks 1983). This raises the question of how much and what kinds of protection children actually need. This is an issue to which there is, in our opinion, no simple, universal answer. Probably this needs to be considered on an individual basis, taking into consideration the maturity and experience of the child, the situation, the consequences of the decisions to be made and the benefits of increasing experience and autonomy. Perhaps it is necessary to consider whether the child, even if deemed incapable to make the entire decision on his or her own, could be capable of giving an opinion or making a 'part' decision, as one step to the final decision. It is also important to consider the consequences of *not* letting the child voice an opinion, make a choice or share the decision-making. The child needs experience and it is obviously better to get that experience in situations which are not dangerous or have very far-reaching consequences. Also, in attempting new activities or practising new skills, it is a well-known phenomenon that the chances for having accidents is higher than it is later on.

A different way of looking at this is to consider the different levels of self-expression and participation. Making simple choices probably does not involve much risk, even for a small child. Consenting to a decision suggested (or already made) by the adult may to some degree increase the child's feeling of involvement and responsibility, but only if it is an informed consent, not one given just because there was no other alternative.

Children hardly participated in the drafting of the Convention. Should they have done so? Some (e.g. Freeman 1992, p.20) have pointed out that other international conventions, such as the codes on women's rights and of ethnic minorities, were drawn up by men and by whites respectively. But, as Freeman says, 'if two wrongs don't make a right, three certainly don't' (p.20). To ask whether children should have been part of the process, or if they would have wanted to, would be the very least we could do. Perhaps the answer would have been simple: 'Probably not.' Perhaps that is one good example of a task better left to adults, protecting the youngest from the tedious, word-splitting labour of international lawmaking. However, if the question is answered in this way, we are falling into the trap that ensnares so many others: considering 'children' as one homogenous group regardless of age and, without asking them, presuming that adults have all the answers. The question should be countered with other questions: 'In what ways could children participate in the development of an international Convention concerning their rights? 'How could the views and opinions of preschool children, school age children and teenagers be secured?'

THE COMPETENCE OF THE CHILD

The noun 'competence' has its counterparts in 'competent' (meaning adept, efficient, qualified, skilled, expert and proficient) and in the somewhat wider term 'capable' (which in addition means able, accomplished, skilful, apt, intelligent and smart). 'Competence' is not an 'all or nothing', but develops gradually, particularly if the child has opportunities to try out budding skills. A child does not have a general level of competence, but may be competent in one area, but not in another, and may be competent to take on a part of the task, but not the whole. We should like to emphasize that 'competence,' 'competent' and 'capable' are more than – but may include – 'intelligent,' for reasons that are elaborated below.

This discussion attempts to focus on concepts related to the development of competence in children. During the last ten to fifteen years, there has been an increasing interest within both psychology and education in the importance of competence, the child's level and experience of ability, capability, expertise, mastery, proficiency and skill (all variously used as synonyms for 'competence'). Experiencing competence leads to feelings of achievement and accomplishment, and of self-respect. Faith in the competence of children can provide a positive foundation from which to proceed in working with children and for the rights of children.

Child-related professions (child psychologists, paediatricians, teachers) have described the development of average, normal children. Using 'normal development' as a frame of reference, the focus of child developmentalists has often been on children who, in some way, have departed from the normal path. Their emphasis may then be on vulnerability in terms of possible traumas, on difficulties encountered with the child, his or her parents or in the feedback system between them – on weaknesses in contrast to strengths. With the rights of children to participate in decision-making now laid down in the Convention, it will be of particular importance to focus on the child's evolving capacities from a positive point of view, to try to determine which choices and decisions children should or can make at different stages of development, what kinds of responsibility they are able to and can benefit from having and how their decision-making and responsibility-taking capacities can be encouraged, supported and enhanced.

Emphasis and understanding in the study of children

The emphasis or choice of focus in psychology naturally influences the observer's perception and understanding of the child. Different directions and schools of psychology to some degree still exist and may serve to illustrate the influence of adherence to one or the other on how children are perceived and understood. Nature versus nurture, heredity versus learning are classic controversies: the question of whether human behaviour can best be accounted for in terms of biologically given structures, motives and abilities, or in terms of qualities acquired through experience in a particular material, personal and cultural environment. Depending on whether emphasis is on nature or nurture may determine whether children are viewed as active agents, initiating behaviour and dominating the world as their natural abilities mature and emerge, or as passive objects responsive to and modified by accumulated skills, habits and learning experience. Whether the emphasis is on nature or nurture also has an impact on child-rearing, on whether planning conditions for learning by reinforcement and rewards or conditions beneficial to maturation of understanding and insight are most important. Explanations of the problems of children and how to treat them will also be different according to the dominant theoretical perspective.

A different kind of focus and emphasis is the matter of what kind of problem one is looking for or studying. An emphasis on psychopathology might, for example, lead to a focus on environmental factors (in the relationship between the child and the parents or in the school setting), which could explain the roots or the background from which problems occur. The explanation could be either in terms of learning theory or, for example, of psychoanalytic theory. The 'problem-approach' also emphasizes weaknesses – in the child, the parents and in the dynamics between them – and therefore may lead to a tendency to overlook or de-emphasize strengths, capabilities and capacities of the growing child.

Similarly an interest in comparing the normal and the abnormal might lead to a research emphasis on differences, between 'normal' and 'abnormal' children, between children and adults or between children on different age-levels or in different cultures. If so, similarities may be disregarded or played down. Because young children do things in other ways than older children or adults, adult observers may have an incomplete picture of the capabilities of children, or too little understanding of the situation in which at least partial mastery takes place. Gilligan (1982), in re-evaluating the Kohlberg studies of moral judgements of 11-year-old children, found that by adding a new line of interpretation it became possible to see development where previously development was not discerned. She says further: 'it immediately becomes clear that the interviewer's problem in hearing Amy's response stems from the fact that Amy is answering a different question from the one the interviewer thought had been posed' and 'in the interviewer's failure to imagine a response not dreamed of in Kohlberg's moral philosophy lies the failure to hear Amy's question and see the logic in her response, to discern that what from one perspective appears to be an evasion of the dilemma signifies in other terms a recognition of the problem and a search for a more adequate solution'. In other words, the adult's preconception about how the child should respond blocks understanding of the child's actual capacity. The question may then be raised of how often and to what extent conclusions about the capacities of children are distorted by the observer's preconceptions.

Intelligence, cognitive development and competence

Perhaps a focus on cognitive competence will reveal a more universal picture. Perhaps children can make similar choices at similar ages or developmental stages worldwide.

During the first year of life the density of brain cell synapses increases more than at any later stage. By observation, experimentation and sensory and motor (later also verbal) interactions with the material world and people around them, children learn the language of their culture, key relationships within the social environment, how the physical world operates (e.g. cause and effect relationships, constancy of matter, weight, volumes) practically without formal tutelage.

In connection with the issues of rights for children, such conditions and others that affect development are important. Brain capacities develop at different rates, to some degree depending on environmental factors such as nutrition or opportunities for using motor skills. Different skills depend on maturation of different areas of the brain. If activities in their turn stimulate the development of synapses, activity opportunities may influence brain development. Gardner (1983) defines an intelligence as 'an ability, skill or set of abilities or skills, to solve problems or to fashion products, which are valued in at least one cultural setting'. To avoid in this context many of the problems involved in discussions of intelligence, we prefer to use the term 'competence'. Competence seems to be the outcome of a process which may have several sources, one of which, beyond doubt, is intelligence or intelligences.

Gardner (1983) identified as least seven 'intelligences' (or areas of competence, in our terminology), each with its own neurological base, its own phases of growth and its own unique contribution to exercising control. While Piaget's stages of development were based on sensory/motor behaviour, the later stages exphasize verbal/linguistic and logical/mathematical styles of thinking. Gardner maintains that these are only two of the spheres of intelligence/competence, the others being 'intrapersonal', 'interpersonal', 'musical/rhythmical', kinesthetic/spatial and bodily. There are sequences and steps for each of them, but the stages in one domain do not correlate with stages in the others, due amongst other things to the different maturation of brain areas. Therefore the different 'intelligences' have different growth periods, and will be more or less predominant at different age-levels. The kinesthetic/spatial and body aspects certainly seem most important during the earliest period of life, and will be most susceptible to the effects of, for instance, lack of nutrition but will continue to be important later as well.

Underlying both problem-solving and product-making is a basic human motivation to understand and be in control of the world (White 1959). The different conditions in different parts of the world will present different problems to be solved, different products which need making. Different people also necessitate learning different skills of empathy, self-understanding and self-presentation. Thus, intelligences – or competencies – are culturally defined and socially produced. Edgar (1991) puts it this way: 'The nature of competence lies in real skills or abilities that are applied in real situations to solve meaningful problems or to fashion actual products that are socially valued.' If competencies are based on the chances a child has to activate skills of language, space, mathematics, music, body experience, the self and others, it follows that intelligence or competencies are developed in relation to other people, and that learning depends not only on opportunities for experimentation with the material world, but also on the social opportunities given children to activate their potentials for growth. Competencies are cooperative, working with others to build, do, construct and solve problems. It follows that intelligence measured by tests for the individual, developed for one group of people in one culture, with somewhat similar experiences and learning opportunities, will therefore not be suitable for people from other cultures. It also follows that the entire environment of the child, in relation to one area of competence or the other, is important for the cognitive development of the child.

A series of studies over the past 50 years have demonstrated that children who are deprived of basic, stable human contact during the first years of life will have long-lasting problems in cognitive development as well as in social relationships. They will lack basic skills for coping in a modern literate society. At age six or seven they will present themselves as candidates for self-fulfilling negative school careers and will often end up as drop-outs, illiterate and with a future of social failure. Even some high-quality education (e.g. 'Head Start' or 'HighScope') in the months or years before elementary school starts can change the direction of this developmental path. The basic problem seems to be not only that deprived children lack the more specific cognitive skills, but also that they lack the feeling of agency, empowerment and self-confidence that makes personal involvement, active understanding and learning inviting and possible.

The lack of competency as seen when comparing these children with children from other cultures may not be as absolute as one might think. As Huneide (1991) puts it: 'From a normative-evaluative point of view, judged in accordance with standards of a middle class society, *a pattern of deficiencies* appears, that is to say, cultural differences become cognitive deficits.' And Cole and Bruner (1971) state: 'If, on the other hand, one considers the question of skills more from the point of view of the children's own reality, *a pattern of competencies* highly adaptive to a way of life very different from the life of middle class children emerges.' Children in vastly different cultural circumstances may simply not need the skills of Western middle-class children, but they may be developing a pattern of skills which is highly adaptive and suited to the challenges they face. This also demonstrates how badly comparisons may fail if they are done without adjustment to and consideration of the problems children face in different cultures.

Yet severely deprived children may have mental characteristics which make future adjustment in a developing world difficult. Rueven Feuerstein and Pnina Klein (1985) have described cognitive characteristics, such as 'episodic grasp of reality', failure to make comparisons, impulsiveness and lack of goal-directed control, while others (e.g. Lewis 1965; Seligman 1975) have emphasized low achievement motivation, fatalism and resignation. Notably, most of the research has focused on negative outcomes. Only a few have focused on the positive resources many of these children must have developed to be able to survive and adapt to extreme life conditions (Huneide 1988; Labov 1979; Rutter and Madge 1976; Wikan 1976).

Identity and competence

Self-respect, self-confidence and self-esteem are enhanced by having rights. Self-esteem and competence would seem to be in a dynamic interrelationship, for better or for worse.

An explanation – or even a mention – of forces within or outside of the child that cause growth and development was often missing in earlier descriptions of child development, although it was evident to parents. What was the force driving the ten-month-old baby who turned away from his mother's breast with an expression that said, 'I am a big boy now, too big for this', or the six-month-old child who pulled herself up to standing, hung on until she dropped, and pulled herself up again, over and over until she practically fell asleep standing up? A two-and-a-half-year old girl was observed repeating sentences with the words 'over', 'under', and 'between' for one hour without stopping, until she seemed to get the relationships clear in her mind, to her obvious satisfaction. What was the force behind this persistence? All these children, in their behaviour, demonstrate new steps of development, moving on to new skills and probably experiencing new levels of competence.

Brazelton (1982) has developed a model for understanding the forces that propel a child along the normal path of development which encompasses the concept of competence. The three sources of energy are:

1. the maturation of the central nervous system, the most powerful and the most limiting force

2. the external feedback system provided by parents and outside environment

3. the internal feedback system that provides the child from infancy with a sense of inner competence.

From this scheme it is clear that internal factors, external factors and the dynamics of the feedback systems between them all play decisive parts in the drama of child development. In our discussion the 'sense of inner competence' must be emphasized.

'A sense of inner competence' is a necessary but not the only part of the process of developing a 'sense of self', which also includes 'self-esteem' and 'self-confidence'. The basis for experience of a 'self' must logically be the perception of an 'I' as something/someone separate from other objects/people. According to Mahler (1975) this perception of 'self' develops through individuation and separation, particularly in the first months of life. Later the perception of one's own 'identity', integrity and value depend on the child's perception of success, mastery and control, but also to an important extent on the kind of reactions the child gets from adults. The child's perception and development of self-confidence and self-esteem may be positive, ambivalent or negative, reflecting the child's interpretation of messages from adults, particularly those who are important to the child. In discussing how social reality is constructed by the role-taking and role-making negotiations between people, each trying to force the other to accept 'one's own definition' (of the situation) in an attempt to realize his/her own interests, Verhellen (1993) points to the unequal power structure which exists when the participants are an adult and a child. The danger of oppression has led, he says, to adulto-centricity, which is most threatening for children. 'It is obvious that, if adults keep using their power to make their definitions dominant by oppressing the child's meaning-making capacities or at least by considering them as inferior, they are heavily damaging the child's identity'. (p.50) Verhellen does not discuss the effects of this on children of different ages, but it would seem obvious that a small child will be more prone to misinterpret because of the limits of intellectual understanding, egocentricity and lack of ability to decentre ('put oneself in the other's position' Piaget 1952) characteristic of the child before the age of five or six.

Developmental level, age or maturity

One of the major advances during the past years has been an understanding that different theories of development need not be contradictory but can be complementary, giving an integrated, more comprehensive understanding of human development. The child is not a result of nature or nurture, of genes or learning, nor does development proceed through clearly defined stages or in a continuous smooth fashion. Development does not necessarily mean 'improvement', but may periodically involve regressions to earlier stages of behaviour. Also, different systems have different age-periods in which they develop and individual and cultural differences between children can be marked. Consequently, development is not synchronized in the sense that everything happens at the same speed at the same time, nor in all children at the same age, although the succession of events often follows the same pattern. Any individual child may be operating simultaneously on different levels where different functions are concerned. Although unusual, Anders may serve as an example. He was 8 years old. His mental functioning was that of a 13-year-old, while his motor abilities corresponded with the average of a 5-year-old. Needless to say, the discrepancies in themselves caused much frustration and major adjustment problems, for his family as well as for himself.

Development and culture

The question of age-groups is problematic. Developmental level may be a better concept, because descriptions of what children are able to do depend not only upon age but on the culture in which they grow up. Many scales of development (e.g. the Gesell scales) have been constructed on the basis of observations of children in a Western society and some of the scales still in use are already 50 years old. The application of Western scales is often not appropriate for measuring children from very different socio-cultural backgrounds, even when used by local practitioners, unless they have been trained within their own culture (see e.g. Geber's 1950s study of Baganda children: Geber 1962). Also, since some norms have changed over the years, even in cultures for which the instruments were constructed, the scales must be used critically or adjusted to the existing changes. In addition, refining research methodology has led and will probably lead to further changes in our views of the competence of children. Research on the newborn during the past 20 years is a striking example.

Age-grouping or grouping children by developmental levels will usually coincide more or less, although differences must be expected. Even motor development is not a function of physical maturation alone. Hopi babies, who were traditionally confined to cradle boards, walked alone late (Dennis and Dennis, 1940), while Native African children tend to walk early (Ainsworth 1979; Geber 1962). Some data might suggest that genetic differences may be responsible for some of the variation, but environment must have some effect too. However, there are limits to the variation: even if Baganda children walk at age 8 months and European children at 12 to 15 months, no child has been known to walk at birth or even at 6 months.

Verbal activity is a combined motor, neural, cognitive and social behaviour. Development probably starts before birth, but is obviously present at birth in all children. The further development of sound production and dialogue depends to some extent on the variety of sounds and conversational verbal interactions made by the caretakers, mostly the mothers. Experience also influences early syntax, but not all features of child language can be similarly influenced. The number of noun and verb phrases per utterance are uncorrelated with any measured maternal speech variability, demonstrating that there may be less room for environmental influence with some aspects of language than others. Also, while there is some variation in the age for learning two-word-sentences, the overwhelming majority of children reach this stage at around two years of age, practically regardless of culture and therefore largely determined by biological factors. Which words they learn and how many depends on their learning environment.

Another seemingly universal characteristic of two-year-olds is (according to Trevarthen, quoting Kagan, 1992) 'a heightened anxiety about broken or defective things, about naughty (punishable) acts, about potential criticism, especially from a stranger, and about inability to understand something or do a prescribed task'. Trevarthen suggests that this change is related to the development of a new understanding of co-operation and shared responsibility of meaningful interaction, and thereby he also suggests that children around the age of two are actually capable of a budding understanding of mutual and perhaps individual responsibility.

One aspect of language development which has not been studied is the question of a possible connection between caretaker language and the decision-making of children. Mothers who ask more yes/no questions ('Can you dance?') have children who use more verb auxiliaries (like 'can'). But do these children also have a clearer perception of their own competence or do they have a stronger mastery of 'yes/no' answers or choices than other children have?

It can come as no surprise that the conclusion must be that it is very difficult, perhaps impossible, to create a universal, precise and detailed scale of competence development in groups of children and that cultural variations need to be considered when evaluating the individual child in any culture or society.

ATTITUDES AND PARTICIPATION

Adult attitudes in relation to the participation rights of children would seem to be closely connected with views on children and on the goals for upbringing prevalent in the traditions and culture of the society. Attitudes may also be related to the economy of a society.

Attitude is in the Oxford Concise Dictionary defined as 'settled mode of thinking'. Children are born without attitudes, but through experiences with the world around them, simple or complex, build attitudes as learned reaction-patterns. The attitudes of adults are important sources for such learning, sometimes expressed explicitly, but just as often and more effectively demon-strated through actions and reactions, or the lack of actions and reactions. Acquiring attitudes very often happens through unconscious learning, without much reflection or conscious thought. The attitudes themselves can be uncon-scious, subconscious or conscious, and the different layers may not always fit well together, they may even be conflicting. New learning can modify attitudes, particularly the conscious and subconscious attitudes, and so unsettle the settled mode of thinking and lead to adjustments of behaviour. This is one reason why information, when accepted, can change the settled mode of thinking we call prejudice.

As individuals and as groups adults have conscious and unconscious atti-tudes towards children which directly and indirectly influence children's attitudes. The attitudes are often founded in the traditions of the culture. But the picture is complex and the expression may change according to which role the adult is in, particularly if the attitudinal pattern is not consistent. Different situations bring out different attitudinal layers. An individual may simultane-ously be a parent, a teacher and a politician, with different views on children in each role. The parent may basically think of children as dependent and needing care and protection. The teacher views the child as a student, expecting independence, while the politician sees the child as a member of a population-group that requires services difficult to provide.

Groups may reflect the attitudes of a political party, a religious faith or the current values held by parents of a certain generation. Some attitudes are more prevalent than others in different parts of the world, different cultures, different historical periods and in different individuals. Under certain conditions such as an improved understanding of children and their needs, societies or society leaders may progress. Under other circumstances they may regress, turning back to attitudes from earlier periods. The different attitude components in a society or between sub-societies may be conflicting, but the composite will determine views of private as well as public adult responsibility towards children. Adult attitudes towards children will also shape the children themselves, in part determining their development and therefore also what the world will be like in 20 to 50 years.

'The child' is here embedded in a cultural context, with similarities to other children in the same context. Obviously there can be greater similarities between children from different communities or between children and adults within one socio-economic group than there are between children within one wider or culturally diversified community. For instance, children and adults from wealthy, agnostic families may have more similar interests than the children, even if the same age, may have with children from poor, religious families.

Understanding these attitudes and their consequences may help our work with and for children. Being aware that the complexities exist may, even if we do not understand them all, in itself be an advantage. Views on the value and roles of children may play an important part in determining strategies, difficulties and how far we feel it is reasonable to go in defending and promoting the rights of children.

Culture and parental style

Styles of child-rearing differ from culture to culture and also within cultures. Studies over the years by anthropologists have shown that characteristics considered universally feminine or masculine can be gender-reversed by the patterns of child-rearing prevalent in the society.

Even without conscious planning, the consequences of parental style can enhance or reduce the possibilities for development of capacities relevant to exercising participation rights. In a Western, industrialized setting, the relation between parental style and the competence and independence of their preschool children, in terms of their social responsibility, was studied by Baumrind (1971, 1975, 1980). Children were judged competent if they were friendly, cooperative and oriented toward constructive achievements. They were judged independent if they showed creativity, assertiveness and a capacity to be individualistic without being irresponsible.

In assessing parental style, Baumrind looked at the behaviour of both mothers and fathers, separately as well as together. In many families, she found one of three parental styles:

1. Permissive parents, compared to the others in her study, exercised less control over their children's behaviour, demanded less achievement and accepted behaviour that was relatively unsocialized. They also tended to be warm and loving.

2. Authoritarian-restrictive parents were cooler, more detached, and highly controlling.

3. Authoritative parents, although they firmly enforced rules and demanded high levels of achievement, were warm, rational and receptive to their children's questions or comments. They seemed to have confidence in themselves as parents.

Certainly not all sets of parents would fit neatly into one or the other category. Little is said (in this research as in much of the other research on the effects of parental style) about inconsistent parents. Inconsistent parents may be couples where one is authoritative-restrictive, the other permissive. Or they may have no consistent style. Or they may be inconsistent in the sense that their reactions to the child's behaviour are erratic or incongruent (in which case, if both parents act this way, they might be classified as permissive).

In general, Baumrind found that children of authoritative parents seem to be most self-reliant, self-controlled, explorative and content. The children of authoritarian-restrictive parents tend to be more discontented, withdrawn and distrustful than others. The children of permissive parents seem to be less self-reliant, self-controlled and explorative. Both sexes, but particularly the boys, were much higher than the other children (except the girls of authoritarian parents) on the measures of 'not achievement-oriented' – they were more submissive and more aimless.

Baumrind points out that 'the same parental style' often affects boys and girls differently, and that the effects of parental practices depend partly on the individual child's personality. 'The same style' is, after all, a very general description and does not take into account subtle differences between fathers and mothers. 'The same style' may, for instance, include more leniency towards the aggressiveness of boys than of girls. Also 'the same style' may have different effects on fussy children, aggressive children and easygoing children, on the tough ones and on the sensitive ones. 'Goodness of fit' between the personality characteristics of babies and parents (Thomas and Chess 1977) would be relevant in this connection. The fussy baby will, for instance, provoke very different reactions in patient, secure parents than in worried, impatient ones. An aggressive, self-assertive baby may be perceived as demanding by some parents, independent and fun by others.

For school-age children Coopersmith (1967) found that personal characteristics of the parents appeared to contribute to their children's level of self-esteem. Parents who failed to define and enforce clear limits of acceptable behaviour were more likely to have children with low self-esteem. Fischer and Lazarson (1984) say that when children develop feelings of inferiority, the process commonly begins with parents who treat their children in a rejecting, distant or autocratic way. Children who inconsistently get everything they wish for and are allowed to do whatever they like may, like the ones described by Fischer and Lazarson, be very uncertain of how they are expected to behave, unable to predict and constantly testing to see if limits are ever set.

In a review of literature dealing with adolescent personality and families of adolescents, Baumrind (1975, 1980) described the styles of adolescents' parents in the terms used for younger children. With regard to the adolescents who have permissive or inconsistent parents (see Maccoby and Martin 1983), these adolescents tend to have serious emotional or behaviour problems, including alienation, a general attitude of hopelessness and withdrawal. Interesting in this connection is another finding: Authoritarian-restrictive parents tend to have adolescent offspring who are either traditionalists or extreme conformists.

Wikan (1985, p.44) points out that child-rearing can have different aims or goals in different cultures including: development of the personality; learning values, norms and skills; development of the person's self-concept; and training in social behaviour. In many cultures information, practical skills and morals are far less important than teaching social skills. What the child (or adult) expresses is far more important than what the person believes in or thinks. Children in cultures like these (e.g. in Egypt) must learn about respect and status, about distribution of goods, about hospitality and rules for polite behaviour such as expressed agreement, humouring or flattery. Wikan goes on to say (p.45) that the emphasis on social behaviour teaches children how to handle people and situations more than abstract morals and rules. These children are exposed from a very tender age to 'the whole range of social interactions, inconsistencies and chaos' (p.45, our translation), and are expected to handle them at an age when other children (e.g. in Europe) are protected, judged too sensitive to handle and too immature to understand such interactions.

In terms of participation, Egyptian and Western European children certainly meet different sets of expectations, and in turn must demonstrate different styles of participation. While Egyptian children are in the middle of social interactions, they are also expected to be respectful of authority and obedient, which may lead to fewer possibilities for giving opinions, making choices, and participating in decision-making than European children have. In Oman and in New Guinea children are very much left to their own devices, that is they can make nearly all choices and decisions on their own. In Oman there are few distinctions between the world of the child and the adult world and children are simply expected to behave themselves. Behaviour is controlled by strong positive expectations. (In Bali, shame and humiliation are common sanctions, even though parents fear that the children may be so ashamed that they will – and sometimes do – run away from home.) Children in New Guinea very quickly learn that no one will force them to do anything they do not want to do. Strength is so highly valued in children as well as in adults that no adult would dare to bend or break the child's will (Wikan 1985, p.60.).

In other cultures taking responsibility is not only necessary, but valued. Early participation in the working life of adults may strengthen the self-esteem as well as the prosocial and/or social skills of the children involved. One example of this stems from subsaharan Africa, described by Whiting and Edwards (1988) Young children ('yard children') are expected to care for younger children ('lap' and 'knee' children). Particularly the girls get a great deal of satisfaction from the positive responses of the younger children when they comfort or play with them, learning to adjust their own behaviours to that of the younger children very early: '...maternal styles in areas of behaviour other than nurturance appear to be mirrored by the reciprocal style of children' and 'the subsaharan children, especially the girls, seem to develop at younger ages than children in other communities into empathizing and responsible assistants who can work with mothers in a choreography of smooth co-operation' (p.268). As described above, empathy and taking responsibility for others are important ingredients in the ability to exercise participation rights. The subsaharan children may illustrate that these are necessary but not sufficient conditions. Little is said about the choices and decisions these children may make. Also the role choices available may be limited in a society where gender roles are clearly defined and more separate than in many other cultures.

PART III

Promotion and Exercise
of Self-Expression Rights

CHAPTER SEVEN

Promotion and Support
of Shared Decision-Making

Children have a number of settings where they can practise taking responsibility, voicing opinions, helping in decision-making and learning democracy, although many of these settings are not recognized as such. The different levels of settings can be seen as concentric circles, illustrating the life-space of the child which expands as the child grows. The family is the first circle and the one which will be the centre of life until the 'child' moves out. The family is influenced by the society in which it lives, so that opportunities for the child mesh and overlap with the circles outside the family. School and neighbourhood are the next circles, which are influenced by and mesh with the outer circles of public authority, on the community and national levels. The larger community is both an arena for children and the level of society which is responsible for many of the conditions affecting families and children.

The following is not intended to be an exhaustive list of situations where a child can exercise rights, nor does it provide recipes for how to handle children with due consideration of their rights. The descriptions of child development should indicate areas that are important to the child as well as giving some indications of how the child can exercise his or her rights at different stages. These resemble the thinking concerning 'sensitive stages', stages in which certain areas of development are more vulnerable than before or after that phase. While few thinkers now conceive of development as passing smoothly from stage to stage, the idea of the importance of learning as the child grows is still valid. Here we would like to stress that 'sensitivity' can be studied for the positive consequences: during a 'sensitive', 'vulnerable' or 'critical' phase, learning may take place which in earlier or later periods may take longer or need more effort. (Maria Montessori based her educational system on this principle.) Accordingly the period from approximately four to five months to around one year is the 'sensitive period' for establishing close emotional bonds to a few adults ('basic trust' in the scheme of Erikson 1968). Lenneberg (1967) speaks of a sensitive period for learning language, starting at age one or two, peaking at four or five years, but with no definitive end, although children at six or seven speak as well as many adults for all practical purposes.

The nature of sensitive periods was first recognized by Jean Piaget. Watching his children grow, he recognized that any developmental progression occurs in a burst of energy, followed by a levelling off and a consolidation, and then another burst. The period of disorganization in the beginning of a new step is what leaves the system open, so that the child and the adults can receive, provide and pass on new information.

Knowledge about periods of vulnerability or sensitivity can be useful in discussions of the development of social, emotional and cognitive skills or competence. Avoiding situations or experiences which are known to have negative effects during certain vulnerable stages can be one outcome. But knowledge of sensitivity can also help in the planning of child-rearing practices, treatment and education. The planning of effective interventions when children are at risk or already in developmental trouble requires the identification of critical periods or opportunities (the 'open windows' for communication) when the parents as well as the child are most receptive. Certain 'critical periods' have been identified for infants by Brazelton (1987) in both industrialized and non-industrialized countries: the first is in the last three months of pregnancy, when parents seem universally receptive to information. The second is during the first months of life when the language of the infant can be demonstrated to engage the parents' (or other caregiver's) heightened commitment. Two ingredients of an intervention that will lead to improved development have also been identified: timing and quality. Quality in this connection means that the intervention 'must be of a kind that fosters the child's sense of competence and fuels his own internal coping strategies' (Brazelton 1987).

These descriptions are not recipes, due to the many factors which influence the individual child's development and the conditions under which he or she grows up. As noted above, traditions will also effect the way in which rights can be exercised. The areas of focus should be familiar. Some are described to illustrate new ways of thinking, perhaps provoke debate on new ways to consider the participation rights of children in well-known settings. Factors that may influence the practical solutions depend on culture and traditions, styles of child-rearing and opportunities offered to children in different contexts. With respect for the dignity and integrity of the child, meeting their needs and fulfiling their rights can be done in a number of ways, tailored to fit the situation in which they are growing up. One way is not necessarily 'the best', but within each culture some ways will be more conducive to the child's development than others.

SOME THOUGHTS ON EMPOWERMENT

In some contexts, particularly in connection with community development projects, the term 'participation' is used to describe how the population, particularly adults, in the community can or should be part of the process of choosing, planning and carrying out a project. One aim is the 'empowerment' of the people, which means that the population, not the service agency or the 'helper', should feel that they 'own' the project, that they have the control of what is happening in their community. This may be harder than it might seem, because when a 'helping agent' enters a community, the structure of an aid intervention itself indicates a relationship of dominance and dependency between a passive recipient and an active 'helper'.

One way of getting around this is through negotiation, with the 'helper' as facilitator between conflicting groups within the community. Through negotiation a consensus is reached about what the project should or should not be. With the population thus involved in the planned change, the experience should also enhance and encourage their faith in their own power to change undesirable conditions.

Reciprocity and equality between helper and receiver must also be encouraged by a mutual respect. On the part of the helper this must imply respect for the receiver's experience and definition of the situation. The helper must 'tune in' on the receiver's wavelength and point of view. It also implies a respect for the receiver's strengths and competence, even when these are different from the helper's.

Participation for and empowerment of children has similarities, but also differences to that described above. As in the relationship between community and intervening agent, responsibility and autonomy has to be prepared from the beginning, to enable a gradual development of autonomy, self-reliance and faith in possibilities for development and change. If this is not done, neither the community nor the child will be able to demonstrate autonomy and responsibility from one day to the next. (In this context it may make sense to discuss empowerment of toddlers. While the very young child will probably have the required respect for the 'helper' adult, a respect for the competence and strengths of the 'receiver' child may be less obvious.) A child or a group of children or an entire community (the 'aided party') may have to try wrong solutions or unsuccessful attempts at meeting the challenge of change, thus, however, gaining experience. One of the differences between empowering communities and children is that in general children need more guidance. Negotiation may be on a somewhat simpler level than the negotiations carried out between groups of adults and the level and complexity has to be tailored to suit the maturity of the child. This may be a parallel to the respect for the receiver's experience and view of the situation described above.

Roger Hart (1992) has described a 'ladder of participation' which has mainly been concerned with participation outside the family, in the wider

contexts of community. Adapting the Arnstein (1979) analysis of adult participation, Hart (1992) describes an eight-level model of child participation. The
lowest step is manipulation, where children are used at consultants, but given
no feedback. Opinion polls and referenda with children can be examples of
manipulation, since young children have varying capacities for interpreting the
meaning and purposes of these instruments and are rarely informed of the real
purpose or the meaning of their participation. 'Decoration' refers to occasions
when children are dressed up in T-shirts related to some cause, may sing or
dance, but have little idea of what it is all about and no say in the organizing.
The adults, however, do not pretend that the occasion is child-inspired.
'Tokenism', the third level, might be a way to describe how children are used
on conference panels, with no preparation and no consultation with the peers
they are supposed to represent.

The next five steps are levels of actual participation, the lowest level
designated as 'assigned, but informed', with the project chosen and planned by
adults, with children who are well-informed, understand the meaning of the
project and why they are joining in, and have a meaningful role. The next levels
are called 'consulted and informed', 'adult designed, shared decisions with
children', 'child designed and directed' and 'child designed, shared decisions
with adults.' One interesting exercise would be to analyze our various experiences with children to see which level of participation they would fit into. We
may find that the levels would not be the same for children of different ages.
'Children's meetings', 'children's congresses' or 'polls for the young' may be
manipulation or tokenism for young children. For teenagers they may be a
feasible way to express themselves. One can also wonder if mock 'courts',
'children's parliaments' or 'children's opinion polls' actually reflect the unadul-
terated opinions of children. On whatever level children and young people have
such opportunities (which can be useful opportunities to learn the consequences
of voicing opinions or voting), it must be made very clear – to them as well as
to anybody else – when they can actually make a decision which will be
followed through, and when their opinions are – like anybody else's – subject
to decision by and through a democratic process. If they are led to believe that
their opinions carry more weight than they actually do, children and young
people, like adults, will either give up trying or become rebellious.

The usefulness of this attempt at establishing a typology (Hart 1992, p.8)
has been demonstrated, because it has already encouraged thinking about the
participation of children on different levels. Looking at examples of the
participation of children, it is not always easy to classify many of them clearly
into one category. Also, there is little indication of how the young participants
themselves feel about what they have been doing. In many cases a description
of the process is lacking, so particularly where national or international projects
are concerned it is unclear who is representing whom and how they have been
selected.

The question of representation (who decides and by which process which young people can/shall represent whom) is a serious one, particularly if it turns out that the young representatives are the resourceful ones who would probably have 'the upper hand' in relations to their peers anyway. How does one then get the opinions of those who are less strong-voiced? If we only concentrate on and encourage the 'born leaders', we may develop an increasing gap between the leaders and the non-leaders.

Another consideration is whether children and adults should be separated in the decision-making process. Children and young people may feel more free to express their own ideas and their own convictions if they are not over-whelmed by adults. On the other hand, children and young people need to learn to cooperate with adults, just as adults need to learn how to cooperate with the younger generation. We think that the younger generation is more willing to learn than adults are. So if the adults are there, to give information and advice, care should at least be taken so that the adults do not, directly or indirectly, take over the entire proceedings. There is need, as Hart points out, to be aware of how children and adults interact. Adults must be able to distinguish what is *child initiated* and *child driven* participation from activities where adults might use children to promote their own causes. Children's participation must take into consideration that their modes of communication are not the same as those of adults (Hart 1992). This is one of the reasons why the media, tailored for adults and run by adults has been of little use for children when they have concerns to present. Even when children are invited to participate, such as in talk-shows, few reporters are able to tailor their questions to suit the communication modes of the youngest participants.

Studies on the 'democratic spaces' actually available to children in different cultures, at different ages and in different settings and how children are able to use them may be very useful as a basis for further development of children's possibilities to participate in decision-making. One main source of information all too often overlooked is the viewpoint of the children themselves. Even research which really tries to put a child perspective on its results often lacks information given by children themselves (e.g. Qvortrup 1993).

A LEGAL RIGHT TO BE HEARD

As pointed out previously, participation rights appear in many of the Convention articles but are most clearly stated in Article 12:

1. State Parties shall assure to the child who is capable of forming his or her own views the right to express those views freely in all matters affecting the child, the view of the child being given due weight in accordance with the age and maturity of the child.

2. For this purpose, the child shall in particular be provided the opportunity to be heard in any judicial and administrative

proceedings affecting the child, either directly, or through a
representative or an appropriate body, in a manner consistent with
the procedural rules of national law.

Also, Article 13 sets forth the right of the child to express views: 'The child
shall have the right to freedom of expression.' Less direct, but relevant to
freedom of expression, are Articles 29 and 30, which require states to promote
the cultural identity of the child and respect the language and culture of the
child.

In Article 12 the Convention provides the child with the right to express
his or her own views in all matters that affect the child, a right that is not limited
to applications only outside the family. Nor is there any age limit. The parental
responsibility in this connection is to respect the evolving capacities of the child
and provide direction and guidance. Respect for this right of the child does
not, however, imply any *obligation* let the child make all the decisions. On the
contrary: it would not be in the best interest of the child to do so. Nor does the
child have a legal obligation to express a view on any or all occasions. The child
has the right to be listened to and to have his view taken seriously, gradually
taking more and more responsibility for making decisions and handling the
consequences of these decisions. But he also has the right to renege, as long as
he is aware of his right and feels secure in expressing any view he might have.

Some countries have legislated the child's right to be heard; some also have
age limits. In Norway the legal obligation to hear the child starts when the child
is 12 years old. However, there is nothing to prevent hearing a younger child.
(The difference between the under-12s and the over-12s lies in the judicial
system. If a child over 12 is not given the opportunity to voice an opinion, this
is a reason to pronounce a mistrial.) In Peru the age limit is 16 years, while
Swedish law states '...and in step with the child's advancing age and development, the custodian shall make increasing allowance for the child's views and
wishes'. In many other countries, however, serious promotion of the principle
is perceived as threatening, particularly for the rights and authority of parents.

The child's ability to make choices, state opinions and share decision-making depends on maturity, but also on experience and access to information. This
raises the issue of what kinds and how much information a child should be
offered, at which age and in which situations. An extreme point of view would
be that the child in principle should have access to all available information,
from mass media, the press, TV, etc., as well as from parents and school. In
principle it would seem unfair to apply different rules to adults and to children.
But this may well not be in the best interest of the child. There is obviously
material available to adults which children cannot understand, and there is
material which parents and others may want to shield the child from getting,
due to the harmful influence this material (e.g. pornographic material) might
have on the child. But if information is to be limited, there are difficult issues

to resolve, with different outcomes in different cultures or even with communities. Who should make the decision? Parents, teachers or the law? Protecting the child is valid if there is good reason to believe that providing the information could have serious negative consequences for the child. But it may be difficult to determine what the consequences may be of giving the child access to or of denying or limiting it. A related question is whether or not material or information which is freely accessible in some place should be available everywhere else, and whether limitations made should be applicable in all other situations, for example at home and in school or through the mass media. Again, where should the decision be made and by whom? Should parents have responsibility for limiting information to their own children while schools should not? Or should information be available in libraries but not in the classroom? Should possibilities for limiting particular kinds of information be accessible, for instance by providing 'chips' for TV sets? Some of these issues will be discussed in later sections.

CHAPTER EIGHT

Why, How, When and Where Can Children Exercise Self-Expression and Participation Rights?

THE FIRST YEAR OF LIFE: IMPACT AND INFLUENCE

From birth the baby has the ability to attract adults' attention and so plays a part in determining adult behaviour, participating in the planning of family life. A wail or a grunt (or even a silence that lasts longer than expected) will cause caring, concerned parents to focus their attention on the child and try to administer to the child's needs. From then on a mutual learning takes place, as parents learn to recognize the evolving nuances of the child's signals (verbal and non-verbal) and the child learns new ways of attracting attention. A wail may not be sufficient, but more continuous crying or banging the side of the bed may bring results. Through this process the child may also acquire rudimentary experience in the rewards of persistence, or in trying alternative methods of problem-solving, learning the effectiveness of each as they produce alternative behaviours from the parents. These experiences also help build frustration tolerance.

It is obviously possible to argue that this kind of impact has nothing to do with participation. It may be easier to accept that these behaviours are at least rudimentary ways of expressing oneself. We would argue that interaction with other people from birth establishes a basis for more active participation later on and that unless we are willing to accept that self-expression and participation actually start at least at birth, it is impossible to determine when the exercise of these rights begins. These rights include more than having an influence on decisions affecting the child's everyday life. The baby also receives and imparts information (Article 13) and has freedom of thought, conscience and religion (Article 14). (When exposed to religious traditions or practices, the very small child is not expected to be a conscious believer. Thus there is reason to question whether some practices, which may affect the child throughout life, should be postponed until the child can make a conscious choice on his own behalf.) The basics of what children of this age need with regard to information are often available within the family setting. In fact many parents are so concerned that the baby might be a victim of sensory deprivation that over-stimulation may be more likely than the opposite.

Article 13 does not postulate that freedom of expression is limited to spoken language. Most babies obviously (and often loudly) make themselves heard, even when their 'opinions' or feelings may be difficult to understand.

Experiences and development from birth will have implications for development of how, when and where participation rights may be exercised in later childhood, adolescence and in adult life. For this participation to be social and democratic, the child must be able to empathize with the other person. Apart from the fact that the newborn does influence the other's behaviour, recent research has indicated that the precursors of empathic behaviour are present perhaps even before birth. Researchers of various schools have described the early interactions between the baby and the adult as more than arbitrary or random, even at birth. Some newborns a few minutes old may imitate facial expressions of emotion that they see in other people (De Casper and Fifer 1982; De Casper and Spence 1986). A mother's speech patterns change in response to the infant's face movements, coos or frets, hand gestures and body movements. Studies of this 'intuitive motherese' show that its physiognomic and kinesthetic patterns are universal and unlearned, as is its reception (Fernald and Kuhl 1987; Fernald and Simon 1984; Grieser and Kuhl 1988; Papousek 1987). At six weeks a baby may show a capacity to choose and sustain preferred visual orientations, for example the mother's face. Eye contact can be controlled by either one of them and they both act to keep control of the pattern of their engagement.

Reciprocity can have different expressions. In some cultures the mother seldom interacts with her baby face-to-face, never looks at it or talks to it. Yet these mothers respond immediately to crying and carry and hold their baby nearly all the time. One might speculate that the feedback system between the baby and the mother is a strong one, but mainly non-verbal, through body language and signals, as described in subsaharan African mothers (e.g. Whiting and Edwards 1988). These children score higher on physical modes of contact throughout the toddler, preschool and school age years than American children do, who shift earlier to more distal and verbal types of communication.

The newborn baby's influence is unplanned and unconscious. It may be impossible to determine exactly at which stage the baby's actions become conscious and more planned. But at the age of two months the patterns have changed. This indicates that the babies have learned something during the first eight weeks of life. Early observations of Bowlby (1969) and of Brazelton, Koslowski and Main (1974) and Stern (1974) can be summed up as follows: 'The infant is an active and often controlling participant in the interaction process', indicating that the infant as well as the adult is capable of matching the pacing and rhythms of each other's behaviour and making adjustments that are self-correcting for the interaction system. 'Exchanges between two-month-olds and their mothers tend to be precisely patterned in time. The nature of patterning shows that it is a mutually generated effect, in which the intentions of both partners are essential, and both may adjust their acts to obtain better fit to those of each other' (Trevarthen 1977). 'The agentic baby of infant research is not only attuned to the environment at least from birth, but begins to develop defensive strategies for engaging in and altering interactions with people by at least the age of 4 months' (Lombardi and Lapidos 1990). Bråten (referring to Field 1990; Murray and Trevarthen 1985) says: 'At birth, or soon after, being especially alert during the first 24 hours, infants appear ready to enter into an engagement of feeling with another' and describes such 'engagement of feeling' in a 3-week-old baby born 12 weeks premature. He also points to observations of peer sociability (reciprocal gazing, smiling, vocalization and sometimes reaching for the other) in children 3 months old.

Much of what goes on within the baby and between the baby and others is, of course, not consciously planned or performed by the baby. Yet the child is obviously aware of what is going on as it is happening. According to Stern (1985) the child's development of a 'core self' between 2 and 5 months of age includes perception of the ability to influence happenings in the world and in people, combined with an integration of learning which gives the child a sense of physical presence, continuity in time and patterns of emotions. Gradually behaviour patterns that do not elicit pleasurable or rewarding responses fade. Also, as experience and memory as well as cognitive capacities increase, there is reason to believe that the child's choices become more active, as inner representations of relational dynamics cause expectancies on the part of the child. The early beginnings of planning capacity and problem-solving are evident at least when the child begins to creep and crawl, in the second half of the first year. Once they can crawl, infants are no longer totally dependent on caregivers to secure things they want. But coupled with this emerging independence, this is also a period during which many children are exposed to an increase of adult control. This is not the first experience of conflict between child and adult. Even from birth, or at least within the first weeks of life, babies who are not carried continuously will at times have been fed either earlier or later than the hunger impulses appear. A compromise may be found between satisfaction of the wishes of the parents and the need of the child. The point here is that even at this stage socialization begins and 'negotiation' is necessary in decisions about such activities as mealtimes. (Stopping night-time feeding before the child sleeps through the night is a clear example.) In such instances the baby does find that others are making the decisions or rules, sometimes overriding even strong opposition from the child.

In the second half of the first year the child, again according to Stern, will be aware that the physical aspects of interpersonal dynamics have their basis in internal conditions – feelings, motives and intentions – and that other people have their own subjective inner life. The child may now use the emotional expressions of the other person to regulate his own behaviour. In the 'cliff experiment', whether or not the child ventured over the glass covering a visual cliff depended upon the mother's emotional expression. Also, children at this stage will signal understanding of emotions expressed by the other through one modality (e.g. face or voice) using a different modality (e.g. gestures). The infant will also increasingly take the initiative to elicit play or laughter from a parent (Hubley and Trevarthen 1979), at times recreating a 'routine' or 'joke' without any obvious connection in the present context.

THE TODDLER: AUTONOMY WITH PRIDE

Starting to walk, being able to reach things and move about more independently is important. Development of language is perhaps even more important. These new skills may very well lead to a experience of omnipotence for the child, who does not yet realize the limitations imposed by lack of skills or by the physical properties of the world (Erikson 1963).

Knowing and recognizing the meaning of words, the child gradually will also understand and perhaps respond to verbal instruction, such as the word for 'no'. (The combination of a short memory span and the immediacy of situational demand may preclude acting consistently on the instructions, particularly if the instructions themselves are inconsistent.) The child will also start verbalizing his or her own demands and wishes, indicating that the child is beginning to be able to reflect upon himself/herself. Language opens a world of new possibilities for interpersonal communication and it is easy to believe that the child understands and can communicate more than what is actually possible. The young child's language is, for example, too poorly developed to communicate experiences and feelings. Also, the child is still unable to fully understand the difference between reality and imagination, thinking and being. Although the child in some ways understands that other people have other experiences than he has, the child is as yet unable to understand the consequences of this. He will, for example, tell only a small part of a story, fully expecting the adult to know the rest. It seems that the child expects the adult to know whatever the child knows, even what the child is thinking and feeling, which is demonstrated by the frustration the child exhibits when the adult clearly lacks this knowledge or demonstrates that mind-reading is not within the adult's abilities.

During the first years the child will start to learn which demands the adults will respond to and which they will not or cannot meet. In a sense, this is learning which decisions the child can make and which the child can influence. Also, the child learns that the adult will make decisions contrary to the child's wishes, particularly if the adult is relatively consistent and communicates clearly.

Self-assertion, the drive towards self-determination, self-control and independence, dominates much of the child's behaviour during the second year. A secure child, who trusts in the basic good will of adults, can explore the limits of what is allowed. The emotional undertone, the way in which mother (and father) set these limits, can be important determinants for self-perception. Learning where the limits are in the physical world and in relationship to decision-making can be frustrating, though necessary. Listening to a two-year-old declare: 'I can! ME!', there is no doubt that the child wants to decide, but does not yet know exactly how much she can really manage. There are limits, even when the child does not want to accept them. Many children want to take on more than they can manage, want to do it all, and seem to believe that this is possible. Inevitable frustrations – and necessary learning – follow.

Power struggles in the family

The adult realizes that there are limits to what the child can manage and the kinds of decisions the child is able to make. A parent can easily be caught in a power-struggle with the child and is able to 'win' by sheer force of greater physical strength. But the adult can also support the budding decision-making, and do so without unduly quenching the child's self-confidence. For a child two years old, the act of deciding seems to be more important than what the decision is about. There are situations in which a decision is either impossible or at least impractical. A child drawn between the demand quality (Werner 1948) of the blocks inside and the snow and sled outside, vacillating between two attractive alternatives (Lewin 1935), is unable to make the decision of whether to go out or stay indoors. Given the chance to make a decision, the choice between red or blue mittens, is something the child can handle, while the choice between staying inside or going out may be impossible. Asked whether she wants to have dinner 'now', a child will nearly as a reflex say 'no'. To say 'yes' would be agreeing, bending to the will of the other. Saying 'no' is a much more demonstrative way of communicating the will to decide. If dinner is already on the table, giving the child the option (by asking) of eating at once or later is offering the child the opportunity to make a decision the child actually will not be permitted to make. If she says 'no' and father picks her up and carries her to the table, the message is: 'OK, I gave you the choice, but since you did not make the decision I wanted, I'm not going to let you decide anyway.' If repeated often enough, the child can learn that having an opinion or trying to make a decision is useless.

THE PRESCHOOL CHILD: WIDENING SOCIAL CIRCLES

To be able to participate in an active, conscious way with other people in a democratic, decision-making process, children must be able to comprehend that the other may have different points of view, different feelings and different reactions than their own. As long as the child is truly egocentric (in the classical Piagetian meaning), there would be no reason for the child to even consider such possibilities, in making his/her own decisions or in accepting/ not accepting the decisions of others. More recent research has demonstrated that the child's abilities to think about their social worlds, to understand or consider others' thoughts, intentions and feelings, appear far earlier than Piaget led us to believe. For the development of prosocial, empathic maturity, some mothering styles may be more conducive than others. For example, the mothers of subsaharan Africa have children who score relatively high in compliance. These children are not simply passively compliant to prosocially commanding mothers, but seem to develop at younger ages than children in other communities into empathic and responsible assistants, particularly the girls.

Piaget and his co-workers concluded that perspective-taking ability develops in three sequential stages, with egocentrism dominating until the age of six. By splitting the concept of perspective-taking into cognitive perspective-taking, affective perspective-taking and spatial perspective-taking, differences have been demonstrated in the age-levels at which these appear and in how the different aspects develop. By simplifying and making more familiar the original Piaget spatial task (the landscape in the sandbox to be matched with photographs of the view from different angles), Borke (1971) and Flavell (1978) have demonstrated some degree of spatial perspective-taking in three- and four-year-olds. As with spatial perspective-taking, different levels of cognitive role-taking skill have been described. Selman (1976) has recorded what he calls 'egocentric role-taking' in children at age three years, when the child can understand that others may have distinctive thoughts and feelings but cannot yet distinguish between his own and others' perspective of the same experience. The child at this stage judges that others will view this experience in the same way as he does, moving at age six to a stage where he can make the distinction between self-centred and other-centred viewpoints, but without the ability to interpret either his own actions or thoughts from the other's viewpoint. This stage has, however, been demonstrated in four-year-olds (Marvin, Greenberg and Mossler 1976) in experiments that demand less verbal proficiency or in other ways are more experientially direct and concrete for the child. In much the same way affective perspective-taking has been demonstrated in three- to four-year-olds (Dickstein, Lieber and McIntyre 1976).

The newly acquired ability for perspective-taking may be the basis for new developments in play, when peers systematically begin to adjust and combine their lines of play invention to create a single frame of play. (Garvey 1982; Shugar 1988 in Trevarthen 1992): A three-year-old playing alone will display rich imagination and create reproductions of dramatic episodes for the child's real-life experiences, but has little ability to share this world with a child from a different kind of home. The shared fantasies of four-year-olds has, as Trevarthen puts it, 'attracted the interest of many researchers concerned with language development and with the grasp of cultural knowledge in dramatic or pretend form. However, this is a field which still wait on a theoretical synthesis, the thinking of most experts being fragmented by attempts to explain cognitive development or the acquisition of language'. Language has something to do with it: around age three to four the content of the child's language becomes more conventionalized and elaborated, with less reference to private, subjective, emotional and context-dependent associations (Hagtvedt 1992). This might be a 'chicken and egg' problem of interpretation. It might, then, be an example of incomplete understanding due to preconceptions that this phenomenon has to do with either cognitive or language development, while the truth may be that it has as much or more to do with emotional or social development, reflected in language.

Five-year olds demonstrate much better skills in cooperative play, which depends on recognition of and adjustment to the separate feelings, experiences and ideas of another person on the basis of a mutual desire to share. 'The preschoolers then enter a new plane of symbolic awareness because they have begun to share interpretations with *a person of similar level of experience* and similarly observant of the culture around them' (Trevarthen 1992) (emphasis added). This description also demonstrates that it is easier for a preschool child to 'de-centralize' in relation to peers than to adults and that this field of experience is one that children cannot get if they spend all their time with adults or children who are very much younger or older. Comparing children in different cultures, Whiting and Edwards (1988) found that there were major differences in terms of how much time children spent with different categories of child companions. Children's culture, developmental age and sex strongly determined the company they kept. 'Nevertheless, when children of a given age are in the presence of a particular kind of company – a particular class of child companion – there are transcultural consistencies in their profile of interaction.' (p.268). Further: 'These similar patterns of social behaviour also result from the shared physical and cognitive capacities of young children and shared dimensions of the scripts for the daily lives of young children. However, as children mature and gain new capacities based on transformation and reorganization of their cognitive skills, they acquire new motives or intentions for social behavior…[which]…diminish the power of…[the similar] responses.' (p.269). Much of their behaviour is aimed at establishing gender identity, practising sex-role behaviour and acquiring knowledge of culturally important skills. Since sex-roles and skills vary from culture to culture, children in different settings will grow apart and girls and boys within the same culture will become more different. The five- to six-year old's perception of the roles of other people also changes. The younger child could for instance see his aunt as a person who could offer comfort, but when the child is older she may be perceived as a 'woman' and someone to be avoided. The younger could perceive both older and younger siblings as playmates, but now may see the elder as an authority, the younger as a pest. Interestingly, in different societies an age-difference of about two years seems crucial. The younger child will try to model behaviour after the older child, but not if the age difference is more than two to three years. This may indicate that 'de-centralizing' is easier when the age difference is no more than three years.

Social competence is first established in relation to adults, in the feedback activities between baby and parents which start soon after birth. By age five, the child is capable of understanding simple reasons and rules, but does not yet know how rules are made. She is beginning to learn the 'ifs' of social group activity: 'If I do this, the others will not play with me.' 'If I do this, I can play too.' The child is (at least sometimes) willing to modify her own wish or her ideas, her right to make decisions, in relation to the social functioning of the group.

Contact with and recognition by peers is something the child must gain. He or she must use language the other children understand. Unlike communication with parents, the child cannot get away with a private kind of communication. So competency at this stage is about understandable, common language communication as well as about social relationships. Play is the important vehicle for learning how to solve the conflicts which occur in role-playing. This type of learning is different from the learning children do in relation to adults, simply because peers are equals. Once a child has gained the ability to decentre (Piaget 1952) it is easier for him or her to decentre to the position of an equal than to the position of an adult, because identification with another child is a smaller move.

As development proceeds, the complexity of decision-making, responsibility and self-confidence increases, particularly as widening circles of activity lead to interactions with peers and other adults as well as parents. During the preschool years the child's ability to think in terms of time and space, cause and effect, also increases. Combined with the effects of gaining more experience, the child will also be able to make 'wiser' choices and decisions, for example to choose clothes with regard to the weather or temperature. Some decisions are easier now because the child has clearer view of the total situation. She knows that if she decides to go to bed quickly, she will be read to, but if she is very slow, there will be no bedtime story – provided that the adult message is clear and relatively consistent. This does not mean that she will always follow up her own intentions, because children of this age are still distractable. Sometimes their grasp of the dividing line between fantasy and reality slips. 'Wishful thinking' can be as real as reality itself. Wanting a toy for herself, she can easily convince herself that the other child does not want it. On the other hand she can empathize with the other child's wish, so that if her own wish is not too strong, she is now able to share.

Experience of competence is enhanced when young children can take responsibility and not only feel but know that they are important. Many children have simple jobs or chores, like minding younger children, helping harvest carrots or beets, gathering kindling. Chores, like clearing away playthings or tools, helping with cooking or cleaning, are also carried out with special satisfaction if the child is working with an adult.

Amongst peers: the sandbox democracy

The 'sandbox democracy' refers to the spontaneous play of preschool children. It is not initiated, but may be guided by attending adults. Even among children of two to three years of age, small groups (two or three members) will interact, although the stability of the group over time is low. These young children will engage in parallel and associative play, and will rarely develop an interactive and more complicated play theme. In spite of this, observations of such groups reveal a 'pecking order' with different types of leaders. These leader types become more evident and more stable as the members grow older. The leader types seem stable in the sense that a child who acts as an authoritarian leader at age three will, unless taught other interaction patterns, also be authoritarian at age five. The authoritarian leaders seem to be children who are insecure, less able to consider the ideas or suggestions of others and likely to respond to conflicts with aggressive behaviour. Not entirely surprisingly, these children tend to have authoritarian parents who are strict and enforce rules without explanations, or parents who are very inconsistent in both rule-setting and enforcement/punishments. Democratic children, on the other hand, seem to be acting on the modelling of authoritative parents who have helped their child to develop a healthy self-confidence.

In the hierarchy of the sandbox the group will function more smoothly if there are some children just a few years older than the others. Also, attending adults can be very helpful in guiding the children to more democratic ways of solving conflicts, for instance by supplying the words that small children may lack, enabling them to use language instead of physical power. In the sandbox as well as in more organized institutions for young children, being helped to stretch towards the edge of their capacity provides children with a creative and positive learning possibility. This seems to be true in learning positive methods of handling social relationships as well as in more strictly cognitive learning.

Nursery-school: learning responsibility

Preschool education is not a commitment for states parties. Many children do not have the benefit of an educational setting before starting elementary school, often at age six. If they do not get social experience in informal groups, they may miss experience that children should have for school readiness. In large families much of this experience can be obtained at home. But particularly in industrialized countries, families are so small and neighbours with peer-age children so far apart that these children may be considered socially disadvantaged. Commitment to providing preschool education should therefore be a priority. This is important because good schools for younger children often are more aware of the opportunities to teach responsibility, democracy and decision-making than schools for older children are, perhaps because schools for the youngest do not have to spend time on the 'more important' activities, such as reading, writing and maths. Perhaps the training of nursery-school teachers is more focused on the importance of observing and listening to children, while elementary and middle school teachers must spend more time in training to use 'the right' educational methods for teaching language, reading, maths and other subjects on the curriculum.

Listening and responding to young children seems to be the key issue in promoting the participation of small children. According to Leach (1994): 'Every time her sounds, expressions and body language are noticed and answered...a tiny piece is added to the foundations of that baby's self-esteem, self-confidence and social competence.' This requires sensitive adults, particularly when the adult must listen to not one but a number of young children. This sensitivity must, as Pugh and Selleck (1995) put it, 'inform the curriculum offered to young children... We use 'curriculum' in its broadest sense to include all opportunities for learning and development that are made available to children: the activities, attitudes and behaviour that are planned, encouraged, tolerated, ignored or forbidden; and the part adults take in organizing, directing, influencing and joining in what the children do.' Children need a curriculum which encourages them to think, choose, plan, challenge, feel valued, to articulate what they think and express how they feel' – that is, exercise their participation rights within reasonable boundaries, set by secure adults.

Choices which could be made available to preschool children may be easy to find, once the adults begin to think about it and are willing to acknowledge the importance of leaving this to the young children. Letting babies six months old decide when to take a rest (by placing their cots on the floor) or when they want a change of diapers (by collecting a diaper and sitting on a 'changing mat') are examples from Italy (Rouse 1992, quoted in Pugh and Selleck 1995). The babies' autonomy and control taught them about their right to privacy and the right to choose a caretaker. In other nursery-schools children made their own rules (UK, Denmark and Norway) in some cases with the assistance of teenagers. Even simple choices, such as the symbol on their shelf and drawer or when to go out to play, often require an attitudinal change on the part of the adults.

Responsibilities may be easier to transfer to children if the adults are committed more to teaching than to service. In some nursery-schools the responsibility for setting the table is a process which starts with taking the cups and plates out of the cupboard and ends when the dishes are in the dishwasher. The learning involved is on several levels: The right number of plates and cups for the number of people present that day means numerical as well as social awareness. The fact that no-one will eat until the table is set and that the cleaning-up after the meal is a necessary task as well can enhance the children's feeling of being important and necessary for the functioning of the group. This is sharply in contrast to the 'job of setting the table', which consists only of placing a cup beside each plate on the table after an adult has supplied the right number of dishes.

Teaching responsibility means letting the child take the consequences if the job is not done. This is not accomplished if an adult does the job for the child or immediately 'repairs the damage'. One teacher had, for instance, told her pupils to bring scissors to school so they could make Christmas decorations. When the children came without scissors, the teacher supplied scissors for all of them, proving to them that they need not take her messages about responsibility seriously.

THE SCHOOL-AGE CHILD

Social learning and social competence

The so-called 'school-age' years, from age six to adolescence, are important ones where rights are concerned. During these years the child certainly moves into the wider world of peers and, to a certain extent, more away from the family. Erikson speaks of the child's need to master ever widening 'worlds', from the microworld of his or her body and the world of small objects to the world of large objects, parallel to the widening circles from 'self' to family to the world of peers. In particular the term 'competence' is closely related to Erikson's (1950) 'industry' discussion, with 'superiority' (with the feelings of accomplishment and mastery) versus 'inferiority' as the dichotomy of development during the latency years (age six to puberty). The developmental scheme of Erikson describes each stage as having roots in previous stages and possibilities for change in stages that follow. Consequently, 'industry' – or the balance between mastery and inferiority – has roots as far back as in the 'basic trust' stage (between birth and approximately one year of age) and in the 'autonomy' stage (between one and three years of age). 'Basic trust' is the basis for self-confidence. Learning the limitations of autonomy is the basis for a more realistic perception of how much an individual really can master the world of physical reality and of personal relationships, to be developed further in the realism of motor experimentation, peer relationships and cognitive understanding in the years from six to twelve.

The focus on development during the school-age years has been on cognitive, social and moral development, and less on motor and emotional developments. In this connection the social and moral development are of particular interest. The theoretical models of Piaget, Kohlberg and others describe stages of moral development that in many ways correspond with and are dependent upon the stages of cognitive development. There is little doubt that rules and morals are of particular concern and interest to children during this period, developing from an individual-based, concrete perception of rules and morals as external guides to behaviour to a more abstract perception of rules and morals as issues of principle, necessary for the functioning of society. A parallel to this may be found in the way children react to frustration. The rate of extrapunitve and ego-defensive reactions (blaming others for creating a frustration) amongst Norwegian, Indian, American and Finnish children's scores on the Rosenzweig Picture-Frustration Study drops steadily during the age-span from 8 to 12 years, while problem-solving suggestions increase. (Flekkoy 1994).

The development of principles depends upon social stimulation, 'the kind that comes from social interaction and from moral decision-making, moral dialogue, and moral interaction' (Kohlberg 1976). Cognitive development alone will not lead to moral development. An absence of cognitive stimulation may, however, co-determine the ceiling of moral level. The bridge between cognitive level and moral level lies in the person's level of role-taking, that is, the person's ability to take the attitude of others, become aware of their thoughts and feelings, putting oneself in their place and gradually being able to take the consequences of this understanding. The richer the variety of role-taking opportunities a child is exposed to, the better his/her possibilities are for moral learning. One of the clearest determinants of moral stage advance in children is the disposition of parents to allow or encourage dialogue on value issues (Holstein 1986, in Kohlberg 1976). Other elements of the child's environment also make a difference. According to Kohlberg, children growing up in an Israeli kibbutz demonstrated a higher level of moral development than, for instance, children growing up in an American orphanage. The American orphanages lacked not only interaction with parents, but involved very little communication and role-taking between staff adults and children and between the children themselves.

There is an increasing awareness of the importance of the learning experiences that children from the age of three to four through their teens can only get in a peer-group (Frones 1987). In a group of equals a child learns how a democracy functions, what the rules for making rules are (Piaget 1932, adapted 1955; Kohlberg 1968) and which attitudes, skills and behaviours are acceptable amongst equals. Fewer and fewer families can provide such learning opportunities at home. A younger generation of one or two children can never out-vote two parents, and the children are always smaller, younger, with less experience than the majority. The children, of course, benefit from this situation, but to learn the rules of democracy – how equals can function together peacefully – children need other children (i.e. peer-groups) in addition to the family. In the peer-group, membership depends on the group as well as on the individual. The peer-group, in contrast to the family, is a group where belonging is not assured simply by membership. A child amongst peers learns when he (or she) is excluded and what the conditions are for joining again. He (or she) can also voluntarily leave the group, even 'forever', with the family as a retreat. The group can expel an unwanted member or let a wanted member back in, on condition or according to implicit or explicit rules formulated by the group. Making rules for group behaviour or for the group's activities teaches children how rules are made, how they can be changed, what makes a leader (which may not be entirely positive) and what kinds of behaviour are acceptable to remain in the group. The individual can also leave the group, perhaps joining other groups instead. Being a long-term or short-term member of a variety of peer-groups will also give varied experience.

In the family, the child belongs, regardless of behaviour. The family offers learning possibilities that a peer-group cannot give: how to solve even long-standing conflicts in lasting relationships with people who care about the child regardless of what the child does, with people the child cannot get rid of (even when he or she briefly wants to do so) or who rarely seriously want to get rid of the child.

Consequently, children need to spend some, but not all their time with other children. They also need time together without adult control. The sometimes rough but necessary learning amongst children, teaching each other how groups of equals function and how to solve conflicts amongst equals cannot be achieved if the groups are constantly controlled by adults. Recent studies of 'deprived' environments (Parker *et al.* 1988), aimed at identifying the strengths of these environments, recommended 'opportunities for play with peers and older children with minimal adult interference enhancing the development of self-reliance, self-control, cooperation, empathy and a sense of belonging'.

Adults are needed as consultants, models and teachers. But children need a spectrum of different social learning situations, a continuum from solitary play (or even boredom) to the peer-group (without adults) to the mixed-age group even with adults as equal members, to adult-led groups and the close-knit stability of the family, spanning generations.

Thinking about competence

Social competence is for many children the 'ticket' to acceptance by peers. Socially competent children have more friends and are in general happier with their relationships to other children. But social competence is not in itself sufficient; children also need to feel competent, have the social skills that are required and wish to use them. This means that motivation is involved. The social skills include the ability to cooperate, share, help others and follow the rules. Asking for help when needed, standing up for oneself and reacting in adequate ways to the behaviour of others, being able to wait your turn, compromise, and finally to empathize, show concern and respect for the feelings and views of others complete a complicated picture. Socially competent children generally are well-adjusted, have fewer problems in school and at home, can handle difficult situations better and are more accepted by peers than less competent children. A Norwegian study (Ogden, Backe-Hansen and Kristofersen 1994) confirmed these general principles, but also uncovered some differences, such as those between girls and boys. At age ten both sexes were less differentiated in their own views of social competence than their parents and teachers were. Children seem to feel that if they can co-operate, they are also good at self-control and self-presentation. The girls scored higher on empathy and co-operation than the boys. Girls also had a tendency to under-estimate their own abilities as compared to adult evaluation, while the boys tended to overestimate their skills. This does not necessarily mean that the children were mistaken, but that child and adult perceptions are not identical. At age 14 the picture was very much the same. Again, the girls were given higher scores on empathy and cooperation, by the adults as well as by themselves, while boys and girls were considered equal in self-control and self-representation.

Thinking about rights

Given the time it has taken for many adults to accept the idea that children should have rights, it may be surprising to many even to think about how children themselves perceive their rights. Children have obviously had rights (although not a Convention) long enough to have some ideas about what rights are and which are important to them.

As with morality, views on rights change as the child matures, from the concrete here-and-now view (what one wants to have or do) to the more abstracted, but not abstract (what one should be able to have or do, i.e. privileges) to the level of abstract principle (what one must be able to have or do), as a matter of principle (natural rights) (Melton and Limber 1992, p.174). These stages correspond with the cognitive development of children, so that the idea that rights are not revocable by authority is not established until early adolescence, when the child develops more abstract thinking. Age seems to be the most powerful determinant of concepts of rights, but social class and culture also have an effect, as demonstrated in comparisons between American and Norwegian children (pp.177–179).

Responsibility in the family

In addition to the research described above on parental styles, family therapists have emphasized the importance of family functioning for child development, particularly the importance of honesty and openness, of respect, warmth and concern. They have described the different kinds of family systems and communication between family members. There is also an emerging debate revolving about the effects of equal distribution of functions between family members, between parents and between parents and children. Growing equality between men and women has an effect within the family, although even in countries proud of their equality-level, fathers spend less time with their children than do mothers and less time doing household chores than their children. Decision-making is, however, no longer the right of the father alone in most cultures. A study in Spain (Casas 1994) indicates the existence of a high degree of joint decision-making, especially between parents, 'in matters concerning the family (64.5 per cent) and if the children are particularly affected in 81.1 per cent of the cases. If the matter affects solely the children, joint parental decisions are adopted in 46.2 per cent of the cases and with the participation of the children in 88 per cent of the cases.' (p.20). Children are increasingly involved because parents see the need for social participation in childhood to prepare the children for exercising civil and political rights later on.

Another result of the study was also of interest here. 'On the whole and in a clearly predominant way, the typical Spanish family enjoys a high degree of satisfaction with the new form of family life...even during pre-adolescence and adolescence' (p.20). Relationships between parents and children remain harmonious and nearly 90 per cent of the young people express satisfaction with the parents they have. 'This high degree of satisfaction shared by both parents and children, is highly significant because it shatters the myth that democratisation of interpersonal relationships and family life generates serious conflict situations which can cause the breakdown of the family unit. The conclusion is exactly the opposite: the democratisation of family life eases the learning process of methods of solving problems based on dialogue and negotiation' (p.20).

Chores and money

One area in which the child can learn to take some responsibility early is by managing money. In industrialized societies in particular, this is also a good example of how responsibility can increase gradually as the child grows up. Even preschool children thrive on feeling useful, on having responsibility. Negotiations about chores or responsibilities may or may not be combined with the question of money. In most families reasonable sharing of the necessary work is expected without remuneration, as part of sharing the responsibility for the functioning of the family.

In some families, particularly in industrialized countries, a weekly allowance starts in the late preschool or early school age. If the amount is small, there may be no other choices involved but the choice of spending or saving. An increase may, however, involve some responsibility, such as providing for week-end sweets or for presents. In other societies perhaps other obligations would be more appropriate, such as covering the cost of pencils to use in school. In either case the weekly amount should be based on a realistic estimate of the actual cost. In some families every birthday means an increase in both allowance and responsibilities, including taking care of travel-expenses, entertainment and a gradually increasing portion of clothing expenses. The principle is, regardless of the concrete objects, that the child take over more and more of the responsibility, gradually learning the need to plan and save and to economize (e.g. by buying second-hand items). Also, the connection between money and work can be learned if certain jobs in the household are paid for. Since many parents rightly feel that children should share some family responsibilities without being paid, only some special tasks, like washing the car, cleaning all the windows or polishing the flatware may be the ones a young person can take on to earn money. In many families the child is paid for doing work that otherwise would have been done by persons outside the family, for pay. In these cases the work of the child, if done to the satisfaction of the employer, is worth just as much as the work of an adult. Therefore the child should receive the same amount of money, the difference being that the child may spend more time completing the job than the adult would.

These ideas seem to be spreading. If the trends now found in the USA hold in other countries as well, the importance of children as consumers is recognized more and more. Increased advertising directed at children is only part of the picture. Studies of the effectiveness of such advertisements (Flekkøy 1988) indicate that they do induce children to select certain brands, either through their own shopping choices or through the pressure children apply to their parents. Children also seem to learn quite early how information from advertising can be helpful in planning how to spend their money. This is an important finding, because children (at least in the USA) have more disposable money and more responsibility for household spending decisions than ever before. Children four to eight years old mostly receive money as allowances or gifts. Older children also get allowances and gifts, but in addition earn money doing household tasks or taking part-time jobs. One change in the pattern is that both boys and girls 8 to 14 save more of their money, supported by savings plans introduced by some banks or administered by the schools. Boys generally have more money than girls, partly because boys get higher allowances and partly because wages are lower for girls. A different trend is that parents increasingly demand that their children work for money, that is less of their allowance is given without strings attached (McNeal 1992).

In some countries the child's right to use his or her money is regulated by law. In Norway the child has the right, at age 15, to spend money he or she has earned or been given to spend (allowances). The right is restricted to 'self-earned' funds, so that the child cannot freely spend inherited funds or funds given for a special occasion or purpose, such as for a college education, until the age of 18.

Homework and school choices

In most countries elementary school is compulsory. The age for starting school varies from country to country, but often occurs at around the age of six. How many years of schooling the child gets also varies. In this connection the question concerns the child's participation in decisions about school within the family context. The issue of whether or not that child should go to school (e.g. when the child is reluctant to do so) usually is one that can be solved by setting objective criteria (is the child running a fever?) or by discussing with the child why he or she does not feel like going (e.g. if something unpleasant is going on, like bullying or a dreaded test), if need be in collaboration with the child's teacher.

A different school-related issue which comes up at home concerns homework. Many children need some support in completing their homework. The question of doing homework or not is by many considered to be an issue not between the child and the parents, but between the student and the teacher. When this is the case, even a young student will be able to decide whether or not an assignment should be done. A parent might inform or confirm what the consequences might be (short-term, particularly for a young child), which may help the child decide. Also parents might help clarify options (e.g. doing homework immediately or later, pointing out the advantages and disadvantages of each option) which will also support the child's possibilities for making the better decision. Many children will understand the advantages of doing homework regularly when they experience that they have to stay after school to complete it or will have a larger load later to catch up. However, some children need extra support so that they are not overwhelmed by the amount or so that they will not work up a new backlog.

A third school-related issue which may or may not apply, depending on the educational system of each country, is choice of subjects. Usually this does not come up until the child is preadolescent or older. Whether or not the situation may involve a conflict depends first on the types of options the child has and, second, on the degree to which student and parents agree regarding choices. In some cases the school complicates the situation in the family by offering choices which really should not be there, such as driving lessons for children too young to get a driver's licence.

In some countries the young person's right to choose his or her own education is legislated. In Norway, educational choice is possible at age 15. This does not necessarily give the young person entire freedom of choice, but it does regulate the parental right to make the decision.

AMONGST PEERS IN ORGANIZED AND UNORGANIZED ACTIVITY

Article 31

1. States Parties recognize the right of the child to rest and leisure, to engage in play and recreational activities appropriate to the age of the child and to participate freely in cultural life and the arts.

2. States Parties shall respect and promote the right of the child to fully
   participate in cultural and artistic life and shall encourage the
   provision of appropriate and equal opportunities for cultural, artistic,
   recreational and leisure activity.

The convention stresses full development of the child. Here are provisions for
the child's cultural, artistic and recreational activities. These paragraphs refer to
participation – freely and fully – in the cultural and artistic life of the
community. Leisure and recreational activities are mentioned in both paragraphs, revealing a concern for childhood and a part of the child's life most
naturally open to their fullest involvement in choice and action.

The drafters raised few challenges to the article, the primary one being the
relative importance of the child's right to leisure and that of the parents' control
over these activities. No one raised a formal challenge to the right of the child
to participate in the cultural life of the community. Some delegates drew the
connection between the role of recreation and community participation in the
development of the child.

Article 15, discussed above, affirms the child's right to 'freedom of association and to freedom of peaceful assembly'. These freedoms, which are appear
in Article 22 of the Covenant on Civil and Political Rights, are essential to any
formulation of a general right of participation. There was little controversy over
the article during the drafting, although there was discussion of why the
freedoms were treated together in the Children's Convention when they were
separated in the Covenant. The major argument in favour of separation was the
need to form trade unions, which was felt to be less relevant to children; the
right to join trade unions, however, was not denied as appropriate for youth of
a certain age (Detrick 1992, p.253). Concern was expressed about the role of
parents and guardians in overseeing the associations of children, but most
delegates felt that their role was 'to guide', which leaves great latitude to the
child depending on age and maturity.

Various surveys have been done to indicate children's involvement in
organizations. A study of US children showed that 80 per cent of urban 11 and
12-year-olds were involved in at least one organized activity, including sports,
performing and creative arts and clubs and organizations. Similar results were
found in Norway, where 80 per cent in 1983 and about 75 per cent in 1994
of the 8 to 15-year-olds participated in one or more free time activities, within
the same categories (Barneombudet 1991). If a child or young person belongs
to one organization or club, there is a tendency that he or she will also belong
to at least one more. That means that there may be a significant group of children
and young people who do not belong to any organization.

Surprisingly few organizations *for* children and youth are run *by* young
people. Even organizations like the Scouts, which started with an ideal that
older boys (and later girls) could be leaders of the patrols, rarely let the younger
members have any input on the higher organizational levels. Troop leaders are

young (or not so young) adults, and the leaders on higher levels are not even always elected. This does not mean these organizations are totally undemocratic. Supported by the research of Lewin, Lippitt and White (Lippitt 1940), well run sub-groups are 'democratic' (as opposed to authoritarian and 'laissez faire'), with joint discussions, planning and decision-making. Many organizations for children, such as religious or other ideological organizations, aim at giving children positive experiences but also teach the values for which the organization stands. One example of organizational democracy at an unusual level was an experience of 'Framfylkingen', the youth organization of the Norwegian Labour Party. This organization planned its national annual meeting so that no person over 18 was even allowed inside the meeting hall. The young delegates had been elected by the local branches, after all members had been trained through weekly meetings to give opinions, argue for their candidates, etc. They also learned how to chair and facilitate meetings, how to handle proposals and suggestions made by members before or during the annual meeting and ended up by electing a 12-year-old girl to present the organization's recommendation to the Norwegian Trade Unions Annual Assembly the same year.

A different issue is the child's own choices where membership in an organization or activity is concerned. Studies indicate that the choice is really often made by the parents, particularly with regard to sports. The kind of sport may differ (e.g. baseball, basketball and football in the USA, soccer, handball and skiing in Norway), but the fact remains that many children join whatever their parents want them to and do not have a free choice. This does not mean that the sport or activity chosen is not good for the child. Many parents do consider their child's skills and needs. But very often the parental dream of having a star in the family puts undue pressure on the young child. Coming in fifth in a neighbourhood cross-country skiing race for four to five-year-olds can be traumatic for the young participant and spoil the fun of the sport. In other instances coaches and parents agree to separate the elite ball players from the run-of-the-mill players, creating a situation of defeat or success for the individual child over which the child has no control until old enough to leave the activity, whether the adults agree or not.

Parental support is important: children who choose an activity and do not get support from their parents drop out very soon. In some cases supportive pressure to remain or persist is well founded: the young musician or gymnast may need more practice to reach a level of enjoyment or may need to stay on at least a while longer because the band or team needs him or her. In these cases the child at least has the right to know why and perhaps negotiate an agreement of time limits or other conditions.

Another positive aspect is that sports and other activities that require fundraising as well as transportation (e.g. brass band membership) bring parents and children together for a common cause. Some have pointed out that parents and children would see a lot less of each other if they did not spend so much time together in the car. The question might then be: is this the kind of quality time children need?

SCHOOL: WORKSHOP FOR DEMOCRACY?

The availability of school is the first condition to enable children to participate in school settings. But many states have difficulties in providing even elementary education for all children. It is a fact that there is an unacceptable level of illiteracy, particularly amongst girls. States parties are committed to providing elementary education, but it is also a fact that resources for this purpose fall short of need. The Convention does not offer an excuse to renege, but does give some leeway, namely that education shall be provided progressively. Still the question may arise of whether it would be better to provide some education for all children or more education for a few. If the latter is chosen, girls will more easily fail to get an education than boys. Such a decision would not be compatible with the Convention, with the umbrella article of non-discrimination (Article 2). So it would seem logical that when resources are scarce, the country must let the children share equally whatever is available, and make every possible effort to provide increased resources.

The 'best interest' issue may also arise in the following context: if a child must work to survive or to provide for his or her family, is it then in the child's best interest to go to school and not work, or to work and forfeit education? In some cultures the working child is seen as being in a learning situation. Through participation in the tasks of adults the child is acquiring skills that will be useful later. In yet other cultures the roles of women in particular do not include the knowledge acquired through school. An education might even jeopardize the girl's chances for marriage and thereby threaten her future. In such cases arguments are made that formal education would not be in the best interest of the child. On the other hand, these practical and role-directed teaching practices can hardly cover the right to adequate education for critical and creative thinking, because the alternatives are not known to the young person.

If there are schools, some families may have the choice between alternative options. Many families do not have a choice, but can in some cases influence the education their child is getting. In some societies choice and influence are not likely, for example when the only education available is in Moslem schools. These schools may not offer a wide variety of ideas, but if the children did not attend them they would forfeit learning the basic skills necessary for more learning: reading, writing and arithmetic. In other cases children receive their education at home, where there is always a risk (unless under some kind of public control) that the education will be biased one way or another.

Adult views upon children as future adults will naturally influence the goals parents set in bringing up their children and the goals society sets for its efforts for children. What goals the schools have, which values the school should teach, which potentials in the children should be cultivated and encouraged and which stemmed or discouraged depend on what skills present-day adults believe future adults will need and what qualities and traits they should have. The accelerating changes in society make it difficult to judge future demands. The difficulty of prediction increases because we realize that shaping the young entirely in our own image will hardly lead to a better world.

If one goal of education is to train students for democracy, considerations of the content and methods of education should be considered in making the choice (i.e. allowing for the development of creative and critical thinking). This involves a respect for the student as a person, with educational methods that give honest reasons and answers. The student should (within reason) have the right to free expression (or non-expression), and self-sufficiency should be encouraged, in addition to offering a wide range of ideas and information. This raises some difficult issues, as discussed above. For the individual child, as well as for the community, this is important because without a proper education children cannot control their own destinies. The degree to which control is possible depends on the culture and the options available. But the ideal of education towards democracy may be valid even if there are various obstacles in different societies. And the Convention can be an important instrument.

The articles on education strengthen the overall participatory nature of the rights of the child. Article 28 sets forth the right of all children to an education, 'on the basis of equal opportunity' (sub-paragraph (b) of paragraph 1). States take on the duty to encourage 'different forms of secondary education' and to 'make them available and accessible to every child'. The implication of having various forms of secondary education can be to increase the choices available to all children. The choices, especially at the secondary education level, would entail participation by each child in the selection of her or his curriculum. Other educational aims would clearly be advanced by high levels of participation: information about vocational education; guidance about vocations; reduction in the drop-out rate. Further requirements, such as establishing discipline in a manner which is 'consistent with the child's human dignity', would also, if implemented in good faith, require input from the affected children. A reference is also made to increasing the use of 'modern teaching methods' – most modern pedagogy places heavy emphasis on student participation.

In discussing the goals of the educational system, as in Article 29, much weight is placed on personal development and training for democracy. The entire article loses meaning in the absence of extensive participation by the students. How, one might ask, can a child develop her or his 'personality, talents and mental and physical abilities' without being actively engaged in decision-making? How might one imagine fostering the development of children's own 'cultural identity, language and values' and respect for the national values and for cultures different from their own without participation? How does one prepare children 'for responsible life in a free society' without participation?

One avenue to student participation would seem to lie in the student councils. Ideally the election of class representatives to a student decision-making body would be a true miniature democracy. But there are many obstacles on the way to this ideal. In some communities student councils do not exist at all. In others, the student council only includes delegates from the upper levels, and it is reasonable to ask why the younger ones are not there. The process by which representatives are chosen (not necessarily elected) can be questioned, as can the decision-making power of the student body. In some school districts representatives of the student council are members of a council consisting of parents, teachers and perhaps other school employees, and in a few the student councils of the entire community elect representatives to the school board, with or without the right to vote. When such things happen, we will often find as representatives students who are leaders in many connections. Even so, very few, if any, feel prepared to speak up. There are rarely ways in which the student representatives can get the views of the group they represent before the meeting or discuss upcoming issues or decisions with their peers.

Learning democracy in school should, in our opinion, be a natural part of everyday life. Small groups of children, guided if necessary by the teacher, can decide how to plan and carry out projects. Whole classes can function as a 'class council' to discuss problems in the class, such as bullying or other destructive behaviour. Children of six or seven who make the rules for classroom behaviour usually come up with rules that are simpler to understand and easier to follow than adult rules are, and the students feel more committed to them (Rutter 1979; Mortiman 1989). Also, when students are given responsibility for making the rules for keeping the classroom, school building and playground neat and clean, there is less damage, vandalism and messing up.

Learning democratic rights and responsibilities in school is different from learning at home, because the group is often larger and the adults different. Opportunities for learning that the rights of others should be respected are better in school than in the family. By being involved as a group, learning to listen to and respect others enables children to understand implications of the decisions that are made and their impact on the group members. Thus, being listened to and encouraged to articulate views promotes development of social responsibility and understanding of the rights of others. Each child profits, building self-confidence derived from the respect of the child's views, feelings and decision-making participation. Even making mistakes, particularly when based on a group decision, can be valuable elements of the learning process.

Experience of justice as a system as well as a value is enhanced when students share in decision-making. But this is not enough. As demonstrated by many students, aged 7 to 15, who contacted the Norwegian Ombudsman for Children (Flekkøy 1991), what is fair and what is unfair is a major concern for young people. Introducing their complaint with the words 'It's just not fair', it often (but not always) turned out that their perception was correct. Why must children go outdoors while the teachers stay inside in weather so cold that adult labourers get the day off? Why may teachers smoke or eat sweets in school, forbidden to the children? Why do adults have legislation concerning working conditions in school while students (who out-number the teachers at least five to one) do not? The issues here were not about health, but the fact that the rules discriminated between children and adults in areas where discrimination was seen as unnecessary and unfair.

There were also more serious questions: is it fair to punish an entire classroom because one student is under suspicion for theft? How can it be that it is so easy to suspend or expel a pupil and nearly impossible to get rid of a very poor or even vindictive teacher? Why are not the rules of the judicial process of society practised in school (e.g. in the presumption of innocence until proven guilty)? How can young people be expected to learn and respect the legal process if it is disregarded within the school system?

Teaching values in school

Participation is clearly implied in the discussion of the rights of ethnic, religious or linguistic minorities in Article 30.

> In those States in which ethnic, religious or linguistic minorities or persons of indigenous origin exist, a child belonging to such a minority or who is indigenous shall not be denied the right, in community with other members of his or her group, to enjoy his or her own culture, to profess and practice his or her own religion, or to use his or her own language.

Children are thus to be afforded the right, as earlier human rights treaties have established for adults, to join with others of her or his group to enjoy their culture, 'profess and practice' their religion, and use their own language. To realize the right, children, even at an earlier age, would be entitled to be informed and to engage, with increasing choice, in activities in all relevant areas. But again issues arise. Should, for instance, this right be exercised within school limits? Should the schools be responsible for teaching religions or political doctrines or values?

In connection with the child's right to freedom of religion, freedom of expression and freedom of thought, the question may be raised of whether or not schools infringe upon these rights if values are taught. In our view it would be impossible to conceive of an educational setting which does not in some way impart values (e.g. the value of knowledge or the ethic of learning). So the problem is actually more specifically connected with particular sets of values and also in which way such values should be taught, if at all.

The value of critical thinking for the development of democracy was discussed above. (For a more thorough discussion see Moshman 1986 and 1989). In accordance with the articles of the Convention, the intellectual rights of the child include the right to use and develop one's intellect, free access to information and ideas, freedom of beliefs and freedom of expression – that is, many of the rights included in self-expression and participation rights. Since the Convention has been nearly universally adopted, we need no longer discuss whether or not the child should have these rights (unless we wish to amend the Convention), nor need we draw clear lines of distinction between the legal rights and the moral and philosophical ones. We may, however, need to consider how these rights are to be interpreted and exercised in different cultures. As noted, none of these rights are as simple as they might seem at a superficial glance.

The issue for discussion often concerns ethics and morals in general and religion in particular. The discussion of religious instruction can serve as an example of the necessity of viewing the issue with consideration of developmental stage and the effects of religious instruction on children of different ages. Social context also needs to be considered. Children below the age of six or seven may have trouble understanding and accepting that people can have different beliefs and views. Religious instruction in the family will hardly be harmful, unless combined with fear or humiliation. But if the young child is subjected to conflicting views (e.g. that his parents believe in God while his beloved nursery-school teacher denies God's existence), the child may have a loyalty problem. Who should he or she believe in and can the other person be trusted? In some countries the parents can avoid this by choosing a nursery-school which teaches their own faith. In countries where such choice is not possible, it may be better if the religious instruction of children is entirely a parental responsibility until the child can accept the existence conflicting beliefs.

In many countries the question of learning religious values and traditions in school does not arise, because the school simply does not have this subject on its curriculum. (This does not prevent indirect or even direct communication of religious values, which may very well be an advantage, if done in a non-indoctrinational way). In other countries, for example in countries with a State Church, the solution may be that the child does or does not stay in class when religious instruction is given. There are, however, problems connected with such choices: The decision is often left to the parents, even when the young person reaches the age when he or she has freedom of organization outside of school. In Norway parents can ask to have their child excused from lessons in the Lutheran faith through grade 9. The child may then be 16 years old and has the right of freedom of organization from age 15. In the higher grades 'religion' is a compulsory subject, so the students have no choice but must attend. The reasoning is that these classes teach many religions and faiths and are therefore not considered religious in the sense of the compulsory teaching in the grade schools.

The other problem is that younger children go to nursery-schools or kindergartens where religious instruction is not provided in lessons, in clearly marked slots on the time-table, making it impossible to provide alternative ethics instruction (if this is an alternative) or to enter or leave the class for the required time. On the other hand it may be difficult to distinguish clearly between religion and cultural values, particularly in cultures dominated by tradition as well as by practice of the religious expressions of one faith. A student who does not attend may therefore lose an opportunity for learning the traditional cultural values upon which the community is based, unless such information is provided in other ways or contexts.

In other countries, with a multitude of different faiths, there can actually be no question of teaching one faith in the schools. This raises the distinction between religious instruction and religious indoctrination. The issues then revolove around teaching general ethics, including tolerance and respect for the faith of others, but also about allowing group or individual religious expression, for example should individual or non-organized prayer in the school setting be allowed, or should religious groups be allowed to meet, and if so on school property or within school hours.

Examples of issues of self-expression in schools

School uniforms

In many school systems, particularly those stemming from the British, uniforms have been taken for granted. The idea of uniform dress at school was to erase socio-economic differences between students and create a feeling of solidarity. These arguments are still valid, if the values of equality and solidarity are ones to be communicated. But in view of the self-expression rights of children, the issue is being scrutinized anew. If choosing what clothes to wear is a way of expressing opinions or simply expressing oneself, uniforms are debatable, even in countries that place a high value on self-expression. There can be little doubt that choice of dress can cause conflicts between parents and children as well as between children, with commercial pressure to buy certain brands and competition between young people as to who can and will wear what. Among elementary school age children many feel that 'sameness', expressed through secret signs or codes, strengthens feelings of 'belonging' to a gang or group. They gladly wear scout uniforms or the uniform of a sports team. In this sense uniforms can be viewed as positive. In some school districts in the USA (e.g. California and Arizona) where uniforms have been introduced, administrators cite a better learning environment, increased school pride and fewer dress-related distractions. Violence in school seems to decrease. Parents have the option of transferring their child to another school if they do not agree with the dress code. In a case in Arizona (as reported in *The Wall Street Journal* 5 Dec 1995), the claim was that the uniform policy was unconstitutional. The court refused to find that the school infringed on student rights to free expression. Since it was closed to the public, the school was not considered a 'public forum' where 'public opinion or sentiment' is expressed. Students could also express such sentiments in other ways, such as by wearing buttons. No mention was made in these cases of whether or not the uniform policy also applied to adults/teachers. If not, it might be considered discriminatory. Nor was the decision-making process, with possible student participation, described. It seems to us that this issue is not simple, but that if students participate in the discussion and decision-making it may be resolved without infringing on their self-expression rights. Self-expression by dress will be possible after school hours, and students may (or may not) agree to uniforms in school.

The value placed on self-expression can be questioned, when, for example, the right to carry a gun is included. School boards in the USA actually discuss whether students should be allowed to carry guns to school. To us this seems to disregard both the young student's need to learn to consider other human beings and the need the individual student as well as the group has for protection.

Organizations

The rights to free association and freedom of speech can lead to the question of whether or not students should have freedom to organize in any way they wish on school property. Arguments for the positive view include reference to rights and also to the learning experience students can get through organizations. They can learn the rules for democratic decision-making or debate, as well as get information about the views and values of the group. On the other hand, some groupings will conflict with values of the society, for example certain extreme political views or moral issues put forth by groups offering information that parents or teachers would prefer students to get elsewhere.

These issues are sensitive and can probably only be resolved locally. In so doing, the decision should be based on a genuine respect for the rights of the child, but this needs to be balanced against the strength of local values and the probable consequences of either alternative. It may be too simplistic to state that such options should be available to children if they are open for adults. Perhaps the opposite conclusion should be drawn, namely that if such possibilities are denied to children, adults should not be able to organize on school premises either.

A WIDER CIRCLE: THE NEIGHBOURHOOD COMMUNITY

By far the greatest number of reports on children's participation concern participation in projects outside family and school. It seems fairly easy for adults to accept that children, at least from the age of six or seven, have experiences, views and opinions on matters that concern them in their leisure time. Some of these reports appear under the heading of 'empowering children'.

Examples of local participation

'Most reports of activities where children are involved in exercising and interpreting their own rights are anecdotal rather than analytical, and more often to be found in non-scientific than scientific publications' (Miljeteig 1994). This is very much the case where local neighbourhoods and communities are concerned. Examples from individual countries are often referred to at international meetings, but have not been systematized and analyzed. Even though child participation happened in many connections long before the Convention was adopted, mention of these experiences is a recent occurrence, perhaps inspired by the Convention. In descriptions of childhood, even middle childhood, and even under the heading 'community activities', texts on child development still do not mention participatory activities, except in organizations and clubs.

How easy it still is to overlook the possible participation of children (and the discrimination against children as compared to adults) was illustrated by complaints to the Norwegian Ombudsman for Children (Flekkøy 1991). One concerned the board of a housing development, where each family had one vote. Since many of the families were either single adults or childless couples, the families with children were easily out-voted, even though children constituted nearly half of the total population. The views and experiences of children were therefore overlooked or neglected. When this was pointed out, the children were told to elect their own representative. A seeming improvement – until it was made clear that the representative would be allowed to speak but not to vote.

A different kind of discrimination was demonstrated by a group of children who submitted the following rules that had been posted in the apartment houses they lived in:

1. Children must not walk on the grass.

2. Children must not shout or scream in or near the houses.

3. Children must stay away from all entrances except their own.

4. Children must not draw on the walls.

5. Children must not congregate in the corridors.

6. Children must not leave their belongings out doors. Objects found outside will be put in the garbage container.

7. Children may not use bicycles or other similar equipment on sidewalks or lawns.

8. Children may not play on the stairs.

The Ombudsman asked the steering committee if all these behaviours were allowed for adults? Who made the rules? How would the rules have looked if the children had made them – or helped make them?

Many local projects involving children concern traffic. Children are asked to map out the danger-spots and often come up with new information. Because of their size, they may be unable to see the cars looking over bushes as adults do. Or they may be unable to get across the streets because the lights change too fast, particularly if they obey the adult order of walking, not running. Other communities have invited schools to participate in local planning, for instance by making maps of where they wanted play areas and housing, and where they think industrial areas should be. The leader of one such project (Fjell kommune in Norway) also points to the learning that takes place when the children cooperate in work-groups, argue their points of view and present their conclusions to the local politicians. 'Children understand that they cannot get everything they want, but they gain a feeling of influence in the planning of their own future community,' says the mayor (*Aktuelt Perspektiv*, 17 June 1995).

In other communities the fifth-graders each year present ideas for improvement of the areas surrounding their schools to the municipal council. They receive a small amount of money which they can use for any project of their choice, thus seeing immediate results of their participation. The fifth-graders must present wishes and ideas from all grade levels, and the coordinator points out that they get results on many levels: Other children besides the 'bright ones' are able to come forward with their ideas and thoughts. The children learn to make their own priorities and find that they can achieve much, either alone or with help from their parents. Politicians see these dialogues with children as extremely positive and get straightforward messages from the children. Even children from the age of seven are highly motivated for taking part in this kind of work (Lillestøl, 1994 Council of Europe)

Similar examples can be found from many countries, for example in the USA (Hart 1992), Denmark, Pakistan and Nepal. In the latter the maps drawn by children were not of traffic danger-spots but of resource areas and mobility (illustrating a child's daily tasks and activities) in the community, illustrating how similar techniques can be used to involve children in very different situations.

The arena of free time activities is one on which culture for children and youth is played out. Many of the arts, such as music, dance and theatre, present programmes for young people. Although these programmes are valuable in their own right, children, if they participate, rarely decide what the performance is to be. A different concept is culture or cultural projects in a broader sense *by* children. Many of these are initiated by children in a neighbourhood, such as sales booths or lotteries, theatre performances or other shows, to raise funds for UNICEF, Save the Children and other organizations. These may be inspired by radio or TV programmes, are unsystematic and not recorded. A different approach was taken over a three-year period in Norway. With public funding, faith in the young people's own ideas and resources, 'Try it yourself' aimed at increasing children's opportunities for creative activity, their own culture and their possibilities for taking on responsibility and carrying out tasks. This would increase knowledge about children and their culture, in addition to improving the conditions for growth and development (Kjørholt 1993). Adults were not allowed, except as possible supports. Children from 11 municipalities participated, writing their own applications for support to an enormous variety of projects and goals. The fact that they got financial support made the children feel that 'this has to be real, not just fun or nonsense'. Even a tree-house (for a group of children or for the purpose of studying nature) had to be serious. Building might require assistance from older children or adults. The financial support also led to a feeling of adult recognition of the importance of the children's own projects. The main learning is that when conditions are right, there can be no doubt that even children who have been considered as outsiders not only can 'try it themselves', but also can show social responsibility, creativeness, skills in discussions with adults (even politicians) and ability to help improve the communities they live in.

WORKING SCHOOL-AGE CHILDREN

Article 32 of the Convention, suitably placed following a discussion of protecting the child's leisure and recreation, states the provisions protecting children from economic exploitation. Work that is hazardous to the child, would interfere with the child's education or would be harmful to the child's health, spiritual, moral or social development is prohibited. Important work restrictions are spelled out without any clear reference to the level of the child's participation in establishing general guidelines or specific individual constraints. Limits include: age for beginning work, hours and conditions of employment, and appropriate sanctions for effective enforcement. Children are the objects of these restrictions and might, as age and maturity allow, reasonably participate in the process of setting, implementing or establishing exemptions to these restrictions. Concerns about the role of the family in controlling activities which might under some circumstances be considered contradictory to the provision, led to delegates clarifying that light work and artistic performance would not be considered to fall under these provisions. The delegate from India, in an effort to explain the complexity of this problem from the point of view of her government, spoke of the need to develop overall economic development levels which would remove the pressure on families that rely on the labour of their children even when such work interferes with the child's education.

One question which is often neglected in discussions of rights for children is whether or not children should work. It is important to distinguish 'work' from exploitation. The work of street-children, carpet makers, textile workers, and young prostitutes are issues of grave concern. Yet these children in extremely difficult situations are demonstrating capacities for managing which at least raise questions: children in the streets, some as young as five or six years old, somehow manage their own survival. Not only that, but 'the number of children who do not beg or steal, use or sell drugs, become prostitutes or sell their companion's bodies most certainly outweighs the others many times over. Strategies for survival consign them to the margin of society, but somehow the majority of them do survive to grow into adults…[who]…find…something that is a little better than the years of vagrant existence… It is because they have to take control of their lives out of necessity that they do survive' (Milne 1995, p.5).

Little is known about the qualities they must have acquired during their very young years to be able to cope. If the child's 'sense of self' is a key determinant of successful outcomes of difficult situations, these children must somehow have acquired positive feelings of self-esteem, mastery and control before they have abandoned or been abandoned by their families, which does not necessarily mean that they have lost all connections with the families. According to the most recent UNICEF statistics, 21 to 77 per cent of these children have some contact with their families. But questions still remain. What kinds of supports do street-children find amongst peers or other adults in their environment? How much or how little contact do they need with the supportive adult at home or in their home environment to maintain the positive effects of these relation-ships? What are they missing in terms of the less responsible learning, the play of late childhood and the role experimentation of adolescence? How do they function as adults? Which elements of learning and lack of learning are useful to them and which are more negative in terms of their adult lives? Could further studies indicate qualities of learning which might be beneficial to children in other cultures? or more about what the absolutely essential inputs are for all children? What happens to the children who stay behind in the street-child's family? Do they suffer more because they lack the energy to leave? Or do they benefit from the fact that there are fewer children for the parents to care for?

For children in industrialized countries other questions must be asked:

Recognizing the value of play, have these children lost opportunities to learn to take on responsibility, for example, by sharing responsibility for family functioning? If their lives become all play and no work (except in school), how can they feel necessary? The small surveys that exist from industralized countries indicate that children of school age *want* responsibility. Norwegian children 10 to 12 years old spend 5.5 hours per week doing housework and theree-and-a-half hours a week caring for smaller children, visiting the elderly, etc. Girls tend to participate most in daily routine work, while boys are more active in seasonal or more occasional work, such as shovelling snow, raking leaves and washing cars. Characteristic for this kind of labour is that it is not appreciated as valuable contributions to the functioning of a household. Often it is not paid for, particularly when carried out at home. (This does not mean that all assistance or work provided by children should be paid for, only that it often is not.) Another characteristic is that the responsibility involved is not always true responsibility. An eight-year-old who is supposed to cook the family evening meal may well find that dinner is on the table if he arrives home later than expected. This could imply that his contribution is not important, that his responsibility for coming home in time is something to be set aside easily. Another example in this connection is 'keeping your room neat', which is the most common task for many children, but can hardly (if the child has his own room) be said to be of any great importance for family function.

Questions like these emphasize the need for more cross-cultural research on the development of competence in different life situations of children. The outcome of such research will be helpful in determining how development and participation rights can be met in different cultures.

Learning or exploitation?

It is not possible to discuss in all its complexities the entire issue of child labour, child exploitation and child abuse in the labour market. Obviously children living on the streets, fending for themselves, exposed to threats to their lives from people as well as from physical conditions – children who steal, beg, wash cars, vend papers or trash, hunt the garbage piles, work in tanneries or carpet factories from the age of five or six, offer themselves or are forced to be objects of adult sexual behaviour do these things of necessity. Often their families depend on their income to survive. It is easy to say but difficult to implement that these children should be in school, have time to play, should have the right to be children. These are the children who in some countries have organized national movements to improve their own conditions. In many countries efforts are made to protect the children from the most harmful practices and to provide at least some education and vocational training for these young people.

Under conditions less extreme than the life of street-children, slum children and garbage collector children, children demonstrate how skills are conditioned by the challenges offered. Whiting and Edwards (1988) describe differences in the nurturing behaviour of children in relation to younger children, concluding that 'Culture modulates this responsiveness (to younger children) in communities where children gain sufficient practice in infant caregiving but are not overburdened beyond their capacities, children are most consistently nuturant.' And 'Again, culture shapes this response: in communities where children are responsible for the welfare of younger children and are assigned a significant role in the household economy, the dominance patterns appear to be transformed from overt egoistic forms (for example, commands to fulfill a desire of the commander) into prosocial forms (for example, commands related to household tasks and socially prescribed behaviour).'

A different but equally interesting finding was that child nurses in the six to ten age group were preferred to the older as well as to the younger child-minders. One reason seemed to be that six- to eight-year-old child nurses are more willing than older children to engage in activities that interest infants and toddlers. In addition, girls of six to eight were more eager than others to imitate their mothers' behaviours and less interested in establishing their own identity than adolescents. This is one example of superior competency and skill in younger children as compared to the older ones. The skills themselves, while not lost as adolescence takes over, must be submerged under other stronger interests later.

Increasing protection may in some connections lead to deprivation for some children. Participation in the work of adults can make children feel needed and necessary, increasing self-confidence and the feeling of competence, from a very young age. One little girl of two was, for instance, responsible for filling a small basket with chips left over from wood-chopping and carrying that basket to the oven. Her contribution was the starting-point for all the cooking and heating needed by the family. Her job was obviously important. Such experience may be much harder to obtain today, particularly within the family, when many of the tasks and responsibilities given to children in 'the old days' have simply disappeared or the tasks have been taken over by machines.

Surveys of the degree to which young people, even in industrialized countries and urban communities, actually work surprise adults, perhaps particularly the parents. Norwegian 10 to 12-year-olds spend an average of 5.5 hours weekly doing housework, girls more than boys, both sexes more if mother is working full-time outside the home and even more if the family has many children. Girls do more of the routine daily work than boys, who do more of the seasonal or occasional work (e.g. mowing grass, shoveling snow). In addition, children take on chores and responsibilities outside the family, spending an average of three-and-a-half hours per week tending babies or helping the elderly.

CHAPTER NINE

The Adolescent
Nearly or Really Grown-Up?

Through adolescence young people are coming closer to adult status, whatever the legal age limits are. It becomes increasingly difficult to separate the young person's and the adult's ability to formulate opinions and make decisions. One reason for this is that young people from the age of around 12 develop an ability for more abstract thinking. They have more experience, of course, but also the capacity to think in systems, in long-range time perspectives, in abstract concepts. Given that they have had the necessary experience before this stage, their morals and ethics closely resemble that of mature adults of their society. As pointed out by Gilligan (1982), one aspect of this concerns the changes in the conception of justice that support the adolescent's claim to equality with the adults and the separation of self and others. However, she says, it may be possible to identify two different moral languages, the language of rights that protects separation and the language of responsibilities that sustains connection: 'In dialogue, these languages not only create the ongoing tension of moral discourse, but also reveal how the dynamics of separation and attachment in the process of identity formation relate to the themes of justice and care in moral growth.' Put the other way around, one might say that the development of moral judgements and ethics relates to the development of identity formation, which fits in well with the way we have seen relationships between personality development and the competence to exercise participation rights even from birth. It is also possible that the separation–attachment conflict may be one reason that rights for children are so hard for many adults to accept, particularly adults who have strong needs for having their children need them. Denying children rights may then be one way of avoiding the tension of separation.

One aspect of adolescent opinion-stating is probably that the opinions are often temporary, albeit presented with great strength, stated to test reactions from parents, teachers, other adults or the peer-group, or to convince themselves as well as others. The preteen and teenage period (with variations from culture to culture) can be a phase during which young people can try out different roles, test values and behaviour, express various opinions without having the full responsibility of adults. They can change their minds constantly without repercussions, swing from one extreme to the other to try all possibilities. Thus they can find out – without having to take all the consequences – which values, attitudes, opinions and behaviour-patterns each of them individually and in groups should adopt more permanently, suited to the roles they would have in the adult world. The young people are aware that they must change; the personality, aims, goals and pursuits of the child no longer fit. Particularly in cultures where the worlds of children and adults are largely separated, it may be very difficult for each individual adolescent to find out their future as well as their present identity. Simultaneously society often demands that they make choices which are related to their self-definitions and can determine their futures.

In many cultures young people must take the first steps toward career objectives, expected to make educational choices which will lead them in a vocational direction. With the present trends of softening barriers between educational choices and offering 'life-long training', these adolescent decisions may not have the binding effect they had some years ago. The labour market also can affect choices in different ways. With high levels of unemployment, there may not be many choices available. Or the young person will decide to postpone the final choice until his education is nearing its end, to see what kinds of jobs are available at that time. Either way the young adult will have a weaker feeling of control of his own destiny than previous generations may have had and he may need financial support from public or private sources longer than anyone expected.

DEMOCRATIZATION IN THE FAMILY

Adolescence is a period of rapid change and the need for making many decisions. Even though the adolescent is cognitively more mature, emotionally it may be a time of turmoil. In addition, the adolescent is well aware that bad decisions (e.g. involving school, sex, drug use) have more negative consequences than in childhood and that he is more responsible for those consequences than ever before. Although in many cultures they may be reluctant to ask for advice or support and oppose rules and limitations, most adolescents are tied to the family, and parents have important roles, among other things as models. In spite of seeming to be on their way out of the family, adolescents can and should feel some kind of 'belongingness' with parents and siblings. If they do not they will seek belongingness in other groups, particularly because, in times of identity turmoil, identification with others is important. These groups may for instance be peer-groups which, governed by their own, often antisocial negative rules, are often called 'gangs'. The antisocial rules in themselves may serve two purposes: opposing a society perceived as uncaring or conservative and increasing the feeling of being inside because the ones that are inside are different from the ones that are 'outside'.

Taking youngsters seriously may, however much they change, be important, because the young people have a right to and want to be treated with dignity and respect. Also, for these young people themselves there may be reason for concern if they are not considered seriously as potential adults, particularly in adolescence, which can become a period of empty waiting for adult status.

Adolescence as a trial-and-error period in transition to adulthood is in itself no new idea, even though it has not always been a practical option. In times when children were considered fully adult at the age of six to eight, such a period of psychological and social 'trial-and-error' was impossible. On the other extreme, in industrialized societies many young people are not economically or socially independent until they are 25 or even 30. The adolescent 'moratorium' can last as long as childhood and the goal of becoming a totally responsible and independent adult can be very unclear, because the time-perspective involved is so long and uncertain. Many young people manage to cope, filling the period with education, meaningful training for an adult career, testing sexual relationships and participating in many ways as adults in society. But some young people internalize a perception of themselves as useless, irresponsible and worthless, and behave accordingly. If the numbers, and not only the sound-level, are increasing there is reason for concern. However, a culturally determined trend of this kind is amenable to change. To change it the situation must be recognized and the necessary actions taken, such as giving children and youth more real responsibility and an increased right to participate in decision-making. Adults must then be willing to relinquish some of their own power.

The extension of the non-adult period has perhaps led to a gradual but actually unwanted extension of the power of the older generation over the younger generation, so that parents have too much power too long over their offspring. In any case, we know beyond any doubt that children and young people, to be able to participate in a democratic and threatened society, need courage, optimism and the will to try, that they will not acquire as adults if they are denied learning possibilities when young. They need to learn how they can influence and have an impact on their small society to believe in the possibilities for change in a larger society when they grow up.

THE POSITIVE CYCLE OF A POSITIVE SELF-CONCEPT

Recently, investigators (Rutter 1979, 1987) have identified the child's 'sense of self' as a key determinant for successful developmental outcomes. It is suggested that children with positive feelings of self-esteem, mastery and control can more easily manage stressful experiences, which in turn leads to more positive reactions from their environment. They show initiative in task accomplishment and relationship formation. Even in stressed families, one good relationship with a parent reduces psychosocial risk. For older children a close, enduring relationship with an external supportive adult may provide a protective function.

A positive self-concept seems to be the starting point of a good cycle even under difficult circumstances, such as deprived environments: the child seeks, establishes and maintains the kinds of supportive relationships and experiences that promote successful outcomes. These successes feedback positively in the self-esteem and sense of mastery of the child, leading to further positive experiences and relationships, more success. The cycle can in this way become self-perpetuating.

CHAPTER TEN

Children in Special Circumstances

PARENTAL SEPARATION

Parental separation, leading to single parent households, and cases where the child is removed from the family both lead to broken families. In general the issues of child participation are similar in both areas and therefore shall be discussed together.

Article 9

2. In any proceedings pursuant to paragraph 1 [includes parents living separately], all interested parties shall be given an opportunity to participate in the proceedings and make their views known.

3. States Parties shall respect the right of the child who is separated from one or both parents to maintain personal relations and direct contact with both parents on a regular basis, except if it is contrary to the child's best interests.

These provisions would appear to require the participation of the child in decisions about her or his involvement with parents who are living separately. Certainly the child falls into the category of 'all interested parties', which includes those who have the opportunity to participate in the proceedings and to clarify that participation is more than attendance, the phrase in included 'make their views known'. The child's right to participate is also affirmed in paragraph three, also addressing the child who is separated from one or both parents. The use of the term 'right' would also allow the child to decide not to see parent/s; most scholars hold that a right confers choice and encompasses the option not to avail oneself of the opportunity afforded by the right.

However, when it comes to the practical solutions, many questions need to be considered. In the best interest of the child and with due consideration of the evolving capacities of children, it is obvious that each case needs to be considered individually. How much should the child be informed of all matters connected with the separation? How much can this child understand and take into consideration when formulating his or her own views? How does one avoid manipulating the child? Should the participation of the child be a matter of assent, positive consent to a decision already proposed by the adults? Should the parents or somebody else (and in that case who?) clarify the child's opinion? How much weight should the opinion or views of the child carry in the decision-making? And what if the child does now want to make a choice or even talk about his or her feelings or ideas?

Parental separation does not depend on whether parents have been married or not. While there is no specific research on the consequences of separation when the parents were not married, there is hardly reason to believe that the consequences for the children will differ greatly from those of children in divorce. In part the effects of parental separation on the child can be a result of reduction of living standards (less money, a new place to live, new school) and changes in contact with parents (one is working full time, the other is not there daily). The primary concerns are the effects on the child's emotional well-being. Research from Europe and the USA (Hetherington *et al.* 1978, 1982; McDermott 1970; Nissen 1985; Wallerstein and Kelly 1980) indicate that effects, particularly long-term ones, depend on the age and sex of the child, the length of time the parental relationship was difficult, the degree of hostility between parents, how the parents explain the separation, whether parents use the child as a pawn in their own battles, how the parents adjust after the separation, and the degree and quality of the child's subsequent relationship with both parents. Most children feel some emotional distress when parents separate. Some (particularly the younger ones) may feel responsible and guilty, some feel rejected by the parent who leaves and some are anxious that they will lose the parent still there.

When parents separate, both parents need time and opportunity to be parents. Even more important, the child still needs both parents, loves them both and should not suffer needlessly from the separation. Parents as well as other adults should therefore try to base their decisions and problem solutions on what is in the best interest of the child. Traditions and values in the society may make this a very difficult evaluation. In some cultures the father as a matter of course will get the children. This tradition may be so strong that the child and the mother may be ostracized by the entire community if the mother gets custody, even if the mother is clearly the better caretaker. In other cultures children have been passed to a relative or a number of relatives for different reasons (economic or educational) during their early years and therefore do not have the same kind of stable relationship with one parent common in Western societies.

In a total evaluation of the situation, the needs and best interests of children should be the governing principle of the divorce process, as well as in rules and services to parents and children after the separation. The outcome may, as noted, differ from society to society. As for child participation, the child's right to be heard, after being presented with the alternatives, the possible outcomes and the values placed on the outcomes, must be respected, mindful of the age and experience of the child, and the child's right to 'non-participation'.

Child participation when the circle breaks

Decisions concerning break-ups of family networks are in general very difficult ones for all involved. While some countries legislate the child's right to be heard (e.g. age 12), no country lets the very young child take responsibility for making the decision. Even at age 15 or 16, when the child's opinion carries a great deal of weight, the final decision is as a rule made by others: the parents, a judge, a child welfare board. Most children are relieved when they realize that the decision is not theirs to make. Particularly in cases of parental separation, having to choose between two parents would be nearly impossible. In terms of blame, conflicts between father and mother or children and parents are often less personal when an outside agent must carry responsibility for the decision about where the child should live.

Participating in the decision-making is only one aspect of 'participation rights'. The right to receive adequate information is perhaps the more important one in these connections. The kind of information considered 'adequate' will change with age and should be given with due consideration of 'the best interest of the child' and the child's evolving capacities. The entire situation and the personalities of all parties will also have to be considered. Most children need to know what the change involves, for example whether the placement in a foster home is intended to be a long one, and how often they will be able to be with their parents following either divorce or placement. In these contexts it is perhaps easier than in many others to 'protect' the child, by evading the whole truth or by 'sugaring the pill to ease the pain'. In the longer run, the pain of discovering that a trusted adult lied can be greater.

Another issue that is often overlooked is the fact that even though an arrangement is made to the satisfaction of all parties, including the children, the 'fit' will change as the child grows. Visitation arrangements made when the child is very small, for example that visits should take place in the child's home, may no longer, for different reasons, be suitable a few months later. Visits every other weekend may be fine for the school-age child, but not for a teenager. Living with both parents, for example a week or a fortnight with each, may work out well as long as the child stays in the same school and can keep the same friends. However, as one child put it, 'I need *one* address. I don't know what to say when the library or my football club wants to know where I live.'

As the child grows, so does the right to participate in the decision-making, and the capacity to negotiate. In connection with foster home placements this reasoning may also apply. The importance of knowing both sets of parents should not be overlooked. With a realistic perception of the biological parents, knowing both the good and the bad, the child will not be so inclined to use a fantasy picture of the biological parents as a weapon when the foster parents deny him or her something he or she wants.

NON-BIOLOGICAL FAMILIES AND ADOPTION

Some children belong in families where the father or the mother (or both) are not the biological parents. Adoption used to be the only way this could happen, but during the past decades modern technology has brought other options to child-seeking adults. The sperm might have come from a donor or an egg might have been fertilized by the father's sperm in the womb of another woman. Egg-donors are also legal in some countries. Also, adoption itself has changed from being an entirely closed procedure to a more or less open one. The difference is that in a closed adoption there is no contact between the birth-parents and the adoptive parents, who do not know the identity of the birth-parents. The child has the same rights in the adoptive family as a biological child, but can in many countries receive information about birth-parents when he or she reaches majority. In open adoptions more is known. In the most open cases the adoptive parents get acquainted with the birth-mother and perhaps the biological father, and the two sets of parents agree upon the amount of information and contact the child will have with the birth-parents as the child grows up. With surrogate mothers similar agreements may or may not be reached.

Article 21

> States Parties that recognize and/or permit the system of adoption shall ensure that the best interests of the child shall be the paramount consideration and they shall:
>
> (a) Ensure that the adoption of a child is authorized only by competent authorities who determine, in accordance with applicable law and procedures and, on the basis of all pertinent and reliable information, that the adoption is permissible in view of the child's status concerning parents, relatives and legal guardians and that, if required, the persons concerned have given their informed consent to the adoption on the basis of such counselling as may be necessary.

This article could be interpreted to require participation by the child on several grounds. First and most persuasive is that having reached a certain if varying level of maturity, the request for the child's opinion or consent will be in the best interest of the child. This interpretation is particularly persuasive since the article refers to the best interest of the child as being of 'paramount' importance, stronger language than 'primary' importance used elsewhere in the treaty. Some states require that after a certain age the child must give consent to adoption plans. Second, since most adoptions require some form of judicial hearing, fulfilling the 'competent authorities' language of this article, under Article 12 the child has a right to be heard, since it would be difficult to argue that adoption is a matter not affecting the child. Third, the final phrase of paragraph (a) would appear to imply both informing the child and, again considering the evolving capacity of the child, requiring consent.

In the preparatory work on the Convention there was some discussion of the issue of access to adoption records, and several proposals were made to add language to the article which would make the records confidential. It was suggested that the records should only be available through judicial order or by other administrative, legally defined procedures. Ultimately, no provision about adoption records was included in the treaty, primarily due to arguments about family privacy and difficulties of implementation in some countries (Detrick 1992, pp.305–318).

In relation to the Convention, and with the exception of older children, the question is not only one of participation in the decision-making process. In some countries the law requires that the child agrees to the adoption if the child has reached a certain age (e.g. 12 or 15), and shall have the opportunity to give an opinion when younger. In other cultures adoption is not accepted, such as in Islamic countries where 'kafalah' is the system for substitute care. Under this system, families can take children to live with them permanently, but the child is not entitled to use the family name or inherit from the family. In this way the question of secrecy concerning the 'adoption' is not an issue, – as it is not in families where the parents have adopted a child of a different race.

The issues raised are the questions of information (Articles 7.1 and 17) and the right to know one's roots or biological heritage. The question has been raised (e.g. Van Bueren 1994) of whether or not the child's access to adoption records is an enforceable international right. She makes a strong case for the child's right to know, maintaining that secrecy is not universal but a Western phenomenon, like privacy. She states that: 'Denying access to genetic records goes to the very heart of child autonomy and participation' (p.5). However, this issue is actually more complex. Van Bueren bases her argument on the assumption that it is in the best interest of the child to have full knowledge of every aspect of the adoption, including all available information about birth-parents. Logically the child should then also know every detail about surrogacy or artificial insemination, if this is the child's background, including the name of any donor. In our view this absolute demand may go too far. It is obviously possible and may be an advantage to have some information, but not necessarily every detail. Genetic records might for instance be useful, if the child should have a hereditary condition. But that does not imply that the names of the birth-parents should automatically go with the genetic information.

It is also a matter of who should have the information when. The adoptive parents may need the information when the child is very small, while the child may need the same information at a later date. Van Bueren disregards 'the evolving capacities of the child' and argues that lack of full genealogical knowledge undermines the child's security to a degree that affects their mental health and that it is impossible for children to understand their own characteristics and potentials without knowing their origins and genealogy. This overlooks some issues, for instance how much biological children know – or want to know – about their genealogical backgrounds, and particularly at which age they start wondering or asking. Even if they do ask and get answers, motherhood is a rule unquestioned, but in some cases paternity may be a different matter. If the child has an absolute right to information, he or she should logically have an indisputable right to know if 'father' actually was the man responsible for the conception of the child. Also, there are obviously many adopted children who can never get this information, such as children who have been abandoned or stolen, so that the biological parentage is completely lost. In spite of this children can grow up to be happy, harmonious adults, particularly when they have knowledge about their cultural (if not their biological) backgrounds.

Similar arguments can be used in relation to other issues of semi- or non-biological parenthood. The main considerations of what to tell the child, and when, must be what is in the best interest of the child, and this may vary from child to child or with the child's evolving capacity for understanding. One other issue should be considered, namely the effect of secrecy within the family. A secret can be like a skeleton in the closet and have negative effects on family dynamics, not only if or when the child discovers that the parents have withheld or twisted the truth. This does not automatically mean that information such as the identity of a donor father must be made known to the child. But if it is not to be available information for the child, this information should not be available to the parents. The parents can then honestly tell the child that he or she is the result of donor insemination, and be equally honest in saying that they do not know who that person is.

CHILDREN OF NEGLECT

In some families children are sexually or otherwise physically abused. When sexual abuse or severe physical abuse occurs, breaking up the family is rarely an issue. The question of whom to remove may be an issue, solved differently in different countries. In most the abuser is removed, but in some the child is moved and placed temporarily or on a more long-term basis outside the family. For children, at least when they are of preschool age or older, the reasons for separation are clear and understandable, and they can keep their relationship at least with the non-abusing members of the family. An issue that may arise is whether or not, at which age and to which extent they should also be in contact with the abuser.

Some families are unable to adequately satisfy the needs of their children, due to lack of emotional, social, financial or other resources. Attempts to provide the assistance they need to be able to function may fail. Then consideration of the needs of the child, for example, for a caring and stable family situation, should supersede the parents' wish to carry on their role as parents. Research on the effects of foster care shows that children who are placed early and remain in one stable, normal home usually develop without serious problems (Provence and Lipton 1962; Tizard 1977). Children who have been subjected to recurrent changes in foster homes or institutions seem to have difficulties of varying degrees, most typically problems in establishing close interpersonal relationships and in the development of impulse control (Bowlby 1969, 1973, 1980). The effects of separation from parents depend on modifying factors, such as the age of the child when first placed (Gregory 1958) and the stability and quality of the substitute placement. As Rutter (1979) suggests, 'children in well run children's homes have no impairment of general intelligence', adding: 'The lack of opportunity to form early emotional bonds to particular individuals constitutes the damaging factor. Children can cope with several caretakers, but they seem to suffer if they experience a large number of changing caretakers.'

The evaluation of whether or not to remove a child from its family is a difficult one, including – as it must – the effect separation and moving will have on the child, effects that vary with the child's stage of development, available alternatives and the culture in which the child lives. But although these are difficult evaluations the child should not, for the sake of the parents, suffer needlessly or too long, making subsequent readjustment increasingly difficult. In some cases a child is placed in a foster home for a certain period while assistance is given to the parents. The child is returned to the parents when they have 'improved', but the added responsibility of caring for the child or other factors may lead to new family break-down. The child is then removed once more, but can rarely return to the previous foster parents, who in the meantime may have a new foster child or are unwilling to resume the instability and insecurity involved with a 'roving' child. This pattern may be repeated, as shown by Seip and Sandbæk (1981), with increasing adjustment difficulties for the child and increasing problems in finding a foster home willing to take the responsibility for the child. These findings support previous research and conclusions that recurring changes reinforce the initial trauma.

HEALTH AND MENTAL HEALTH

A superficial look at health issues can easily lead to the conclusion that children do not have any choice, cannot make decisions and hardly need to voice opinions, because these would be useless or worthless anyway. However, health issues have been discussed more often than many other issues, particularly the question of when consent from the child should be obtained.

Health issues range from life-and-death decisions to the choices possible regarding everyday life, such as what to eat for a nutritious diet. Toddlers can choose between two fruits or vegetables and should probably not be given the chance to choose whether or not they will eat vegetables or fruit, even though some research seems to indicate that the total diet of a child, given free choices, will over a several-week period be balanced. In many cases small children can choose between simple options, but in many cases there is no reason to offer choices which would lead to unfortunate results. In the best interest of the child, vaccinations need to be administered. Given a chance, the small child may very well protest. To give the child some control, other alternatives may be offered, for example whether the shot should be given in the left or the right arm, or perhaps in the thigh. It may be argued that this is an example of obtaining 'consent' or compliance through offering some liberty of choice. In our opinion this is acceptable when the strategy, even if manipulative, serves the best interest of the child. We can, however, understand the argument and therefore emphasize that it must *really* be in the best interest of the child.

In more serious situations, and the more so the older the child, the issue of consent or choice can be more pressing. Two conditions must then be fulfilled: There must be a real choice between realistic alternatives to be made and the child must be competent to understand and evaluate the information given about the alternatives, perhaps long-term as well as short-term consequences. 'A real choice' means that no single alternative is clearly better than the other.

Judgement of the amount of information to give and how to do it obviously varies with the maturity of the child or young person, but the type and seriousness of the condition can also influence the decision. In our view honesty is a basic requirement, but that does not mean that all information, all possibilities need to be clarified to the patient, at least not all at once. Some possible pitfalls make these issues even more difficult, such as the possibility of manipulating the child by omitting information about existing options, or a very understandable wish to protect the child from painful considerations. Should a child for instance be told that death is a possible or probable outcome, even after long-term and painful therapy? And who should give the child the information? Many professionals let the parents choose whether they want to do this or leave it to doctors or nurses. Experience indicates, however, that the parents in most cases at least should be present, so that the child knows that the parents know what has been said. It appears that this helps the child share thoughts and feelings about the situation, even when it is a dire one, and also to discuss wishes the child may have, such as making a will or consenting to organ donation. (Even young children can understand and be happy to help other children in this way, morbid as it may seem to adults to discuss this option with their children.)

In some cases one alternative may be institutionalizing a child or young person at least for a period of time. Depriving a child or young person of his or her liberty, for example in a psychiatric setting for treatment, may be in the best interest of the child. The very conditions of the patient may cause lack of understanding and of consent, not to mention a positive decision to get such help. The question of at which age consent to psychiatric treatment should be a requirement has been raised but, in our view, not clarified in a satisfactory way.

There are situations where the lack of required consent would deny the patient needed treatment, either because the child is too young, too confused or otherwise mentally disturbed in such a way that he or she is unable to comprehend and agree to treatment. Also, some treatments are so painful to the patient that he or she may object, even if the outcome is one wished for, for instance in cases of drug abuse. Enforcement of treatment may therefore be the only option. In such cases a minimum requirement must be that the child or young person, while perhaps denied liberty of movement, is not denied other rights, such as the right to information, and that other needs are satisfied, for example the need to stay in touch with parents.

DELINQUENCY AND CRIME

Article 37 concerns, among other issues, deprivation of liberty and prohibition of cruel treatment or punishment:

> States Parties shall ensure that:
>
> (a) No child shall be subjected to torture or other cruel, inhuman or degrading treatment or punishment, Neither capital punishment nor life imprisonment without possibility of release shall be imposed for offences committed by persons below 18 years of age;
>
> (b) No child shall be deprived of his or her liberty unlawfully or arbitrarily. The arrest, detention or imprisonment of a child shall be in conformity with the law and shall be used only as a measure of last resort and for the shortest appropriate period of time;
>
> (c) Every child deprived of liberty shall be treated with humanity and respect for the inherent dignity of the human person, and in a manner which takes into account the needs of persons of their age.

Observations similar to those made above concerning institutionalization of children also arise when the institution in question is a prison or other type of incarceration of young delinquents. In this context even general observations are particularly difficult, because the legal systems vary so much from country to country. In some countries even elementary school-age children can be imprisoned if the crime is very serious. In other countries no-one under a certain age, for instance 14 or 16, can be put in prison even overnight. In spite of ratifying the Convention and therefore agreeing to the principle of special treatment for young offenders, many countries in practice and some in principle do not comply with this article. In the UK eight- and ten-year-olds are serving long sentences in jail. In Norway this would not happen. Even after taking the life of another child, children this young would be transferred to the child welfare and child psychiatric systems for treatment. In spite of this, one Norwegian reservation to the Convention was precisely concerning this article. The reasons were, however, in the best interest of the child. Norway is a country with a small and very sparse population. Special facilities for young offenders would cut off the possibilities these young people need to stay in touch with their friends and families.

These examples illustrate that treatment of young offenders depends on geography, but even more on the legislation, philosophy and types of systems a country has regarding this group. Some countries have special juvenile courts, others do not. Some have child welfare and treatment facilities that are not available – or even wanted – in other countries. Finally, views differ on what types of behaviour actually are defined as illegal, as a crime or as a less serious offence. In addition, different legal systems must be viewed in the context of other systems, for example child welfare.

With these reservations in mind, we need to stress the humane principle of Article 37 and also that prevention should be considered far more important than punishment or revenge (which is often the basis for punishment). The whole issue of juvenile offences within society highlights the weaknesses of many communities, such as lack of positive and creative groups to which young people can belong. Adolescents' need to feel belongingness combined with the need many have to oppose (at least for a time) the values and morals of parents and other adults make them particularly vulnerable to invitations from criminal groups or gangs if other, more positive alternatives are missing.

Discussions about prevention may need to focus on what happens when and if children growing up are deprived of learning to take responsibility and the experiences of taking the consequences for their actions and behaviour. Discussions about societal reactions to misbehaviour, such as vandalism, shop-lifting, car thefts and other fairly common misdeeds done by young people individually and in groups, may need to focus on teaching rather than punishing. In some countries first offences lead to confrontations with the victim (e.g. the owner of the building, shop or car) with an arbitrator, the goal being to find some method of restitution. The young person may, for instance, clean up the mess, work in the shop or take a job to repay the repair of the car. These confrontations mean that the young person gets a personal, first-hand impression of the emotional as well as the economic effects of the offence, a chance to make 'repairs' (which must be considered more positive than revenge) and the possibility of avoiding a police record. The results thus far seem to indicate that very few of these young people have later arrests for misdemeaners or offences. Where such systems exist, an opportunity for choice, for participating in the decision-making, also exists, in contrast to the lack of such possible options elsewhere within the legal system.

CHAPTER ELEVEN

Concluding Remarks

PUBLIC OBLIGATIONS TO THE CHILD

Public responsibility for children has been recognized for centuries. The Convention emphasizes these obligations, but frequently in terms that weaken them. For example, words such as 'to the maximum extent of their available resources' (Article 4.2), 'to the maximum extent possible' (Art 6.2) and 'the highest attainable standard' (Article 23.1) reflect recognition that resources are not always available, leaving each state party with the responsibility of defending the standard achieved. Some changes in society are so gradual that it takes time to see the consequences for children and then do something to compensate for losses or prevent negative effects. One example of this, found in many countries, is the consequences for children of the changing family. In Europe about 50 years ago the average child had 3 or 4 siblings, 65 to 70 cousins and 14 aunts or uncles. Now the average child has one sibling, 3 or 4 cousins and 3 aunts or uncles. One consequence is that the group within which a child can learn how a democracy works is too small to serve this purpose. Other opportunities to interact simultaneously with older and younger peers can be hard to find. Even in schools the children are grouped according to age.

A different example is the conviction found in many adults that children can play safely out of doors. Realization that safe play areas have been destroyed or made unreachable by traffic or buildings is slow and changing this by providing or protecting such areas can be even slower.

One way the state can fulfil its obligations to children is by adopting legislation to secure their rights and conditions. As discussed above, such legislation can be reactive or proactive. The proactive legislation to ensure education, health services and rights for parents which will be beneficial to the child (such as leave when a child is born or ill, working hours to suit the family, financial support to families) is often expensive, at least in the short run. Research (e.g. Weikart *et al.* 1978) indicates that in the long run the money spent for quality preschool education is returned 5 to 7-fold in the course of the next 20 years. Young people with this experience do not need as much special education assistance, do not drop out of school, commit criminal acts or need unemployment assistance as often as young people without the early education opportunity. We lack studies of this kind, which is a great pity because politicians tend to think in terms of 4 to 6 years (election terms). They need to learn that planning for children should be done in terms of 10 to 20 years.

Other proactive legislation does not cost much, such as legislation to protect the child from corporal punishment. The value of legislation depends not only on the cost, even though many feel that such issues as the right to education should not be legislated until resources are actually available. Attitudes towards politicians and parliament also make a difference. In some countries there is a high disregard for national legislation because the people feel that the politicians are too far away or that the legislation cannot be enforced so it can be disregarded.

In connection with the Convention, the legislators need to know what the legal status of a Convention is and how national legislation needs to be amended, if at all, to fit the obligations of the Convention. For example in some countries the right to adequate information should lead to national legislation prohibiting or controlling TV violence. There can be no doubt that TV and video violence can have negative effects on children. Where the private or commercial TV and video companies are unwilling to control this themselves, national rules or laws should be considered. A parallel can be found in the national guidelines accepted by toy sellers to limit sales of war-toys. These guidelines do not, however, include guns and other arms used in wars of the future shown on TV, nor video games or software programmes with violent (or pornographic) content. In Sweden the Parliament has therefore recommended that the producers and distributors take responsibility for 'cleaning up their act'. If this does not have the required effect, Parliament will consider the need for prohibitive legislation.

Participation rights need to be protected and encouraged. The states parties also have an obligation to make the Convention known to children. Consideration of measures to encourage participation should also include initiatives to give children a voice. On the state level that might involve establishment of an Ombudsman for Children or similar mechanism.

ATTITUDES SHAPE CHILDREN

Children need to acquire the skills and competencies that will prepare them for a wide variety of possible futures. Communications skills and social skills will be important regardless of how societies develop. Future adults will need persistence and courage, flexibility and creativity, self-confidence and responsibility, as well as imagination and faith. One way to give them this is by believing in children, by trusting in the evolving competence of children. Children who are active in decision-making, who learn from their own experience as well as by seeing adults spending time and energy involved in 'causes', because they believe they can contribute to making a change, are less prone to depression, hopelessness and suicide (Escalona 1982; Raundalen and Raundalen 1984; Schwebel 1982). Starting with having some impact in their own families, learning that they can make a difference in the neighbourhood, in their organizations and in schools, children's faith in the possibilities for change, their courage to try and their persistence in the face of the odds grows with them. This encourages development of personality characteristics important in any future society, particularly as the need to cooperate with people of different cultural backgrounds increases.

Adult responsibility in relation to these rights would include ensuring ample opportunities for developing the necessary skills and expressing these rights according to ability. We must learn more about how these abilities are learned, under which conditions, and thus which decisions children could make as a consequence of new learning opportunities.

Adults also need to be aware of the importance of information from the young citizens themselves. Only children can help to identify those issues which are of most concern to children themselves. These issues may not be the ones identified by adults, even in situations that both children and adults will say are difficult. In divorce, for instance, children rarely identify the divorce itself as the worst part, but more everyday worries, like moving from one parent to the other or having to work out agreements about visitation. By asking children themselves about how they see their rights and the ways in which these rights can be exercised, information can be obtained about necessary steps needed for implementation of rights in ways children can handle (e.g. the establishment of an Ombudsman for Children, as in Norway and some other countries). A third reason to ask children about their rights is that this can be a strong signal to the children that they and their views are taken seriously. Finally, and perhaps most important, systematic involvement of children can have socializing effects on the child, and also have an impact on their views of the future. As will be described below, this should be of major importance to the future of the world, because participation fosters democratic principles and practices.

Adult attitudes towards children – as individuals and as a group – will influence the children and their development. In any interaction between children and adults there is a continuous feedback system of interpretation of behaviour, with the child adjusting behaviour according to what the child perceives as important to the adult, and the adult adjusting to what is perceived as the child's needs. That is how values, attitudes and roles of the growing person are learned and developed. That is why it is so important to change the attitudes of adults when and if necessary. The signals come from many sources – first, mostly from the parents. But as the child grows other adults (teachers and organization leaders) gain importance, as do other children and the signals from mass media, particularly television, including advertising. The communications about values found in mass media are often contradictory to the values of parents and teachers, but the authorities or persons responsible often do not seem willing to introduce the measures which could protect the children. This might serve as one example of a more general discrepancy between professed attitudes and action, the attitudes expressed in principle being that children are important, the actions showing them that this is not true. For example, if we maintain that schools are important but let the children get their education in run-down buildings, with tattered books and out-dated information, how can we expect children in countries that could obviously afford better to respect school property and feel that they – as pupils – are important? When youth-clubs and leisure-time facilities, school-transportation and health-services are the first projects to be obliterated when local economy is tight, how can children believe that their lives and activities are important? Slogans such as 'Children are our most valuable asset' are not worth much when society does not seriously realize its responsibility for children.

For parents the child as an individual, as a member of the family, as emotionally important, carries most weight. For society the importance of children as future adults perhaps carries more weight. Children and youth as active, participating members of groups, with opinions worth listening to, have not been considered important enough. The UN Convention may change attitudes and provide new ways of thinking about and perceiving children. Already, in emphasizing that children can act as their own people, having rights of participation, the Convention is providing a new view of children. Children are supposed to be active in implementing the Convention. This is a Convention which is not to be implemented only *for* children, but *by* them as well. And they have already demonstrated that they want to do it and can do it. The examples described above give ample evidence that, when given the opportunity, children have the competence to make a real difference. This is particularly true in the family and within the local community. Even if children can influence national or international policies, the grass-roots level, where they spend their time, is probably the most important level of participation. On this level they can be actively involved in improving their conditions and thereby implementing their own rights, such as to better health or safe-play areas.

The next generations of adults must be brought up to respect the integrity and dignity of all other human beings, including the small ones, as equal although different from themselves. In exercising participation rights they are learning the general rules of human rights as well as of democracy. That should give hope for the future. Looking at the value of children in a global perspective, it is obvious that the world needs children, but not only because children represent our future. Children are also the embodiment of global values. Therefore children do not divide but unite peoples or countries. They embody as well certain global duties and they are the indicators of what the world needs. Recognition of the needs and situation of children should bridge the gap between East and West, North and South. And, finally, children are the hope of the future also because they give purpose and meaning to life when ideologies crumble, when despair threatens to overwhelm us, when everything else seems to fail.

Appendix 1. Survey of Legal Age Limits

Country	Compulsory school age	Minimum age for employment (light/heavy labour)	Minimum age for imprisonment	Minimum age to marry		Minimum age for political rights	
				men	women	To vote	To be elected
Austria	6–15	15	14	19	16	19	21
Bangladesh	not compulsory					18	18
Bulgaria		7–14	16	18	18	18	18
Canada	6–15	15	14/16	14	14	18	21
Chile	6–15	15	16	21	21	21	18
Colombia	7–11	14	16	21	21	18	18
Costa Rica	6–14	12/15	16	18	18	18	21
Denmark	7–16	15	15	18	18	18	18
Finland	7–16	15	15	18	17	18	18
France	6–16	16	13	18	15	18	18
Germany, F.R.	6–15	15	14	21	18	18	18
India	6–11	12/15	16	21	18	21	21
Italy	6–14	14/15	14	18/16	18/16	18	18/25
Jamaica	6–17	12/15	14	18	18	18	18
Japan	6–15	15	15	18	15	18	25
Morocco	not compulsory	12	12/16	18	15	21	25
Netherlands	6–16	15	16	18	18	18	18
Nigeria	6–11	12	12	12	12	18	18
Pakistan	not compulsory	12/10	12	18	18	21	23
Romania	6–16	16	14	18	16/15	18	23
South Africa	7–14	none	7/10	16/15	16/15	18	18
Spain	6–15	16	16	18	18	18	18
Switzerland	6–15	15	15	18	18	20	18
Thailand	7–15	none	16	16	16	18	18
United Kingdom	5–16	16	14	16	16	18	21
United States	7–16	16		18	16	18	21
Yugoslavia	7–15	15	16	18	18	18	18
Zaire	6–11	16	16	18	18	18	18

Source: the data are taken from UNESCO Yearbooks, information supplied by the ILO on the implementation of its conventions and recommendations and states reports to on the implementation of Human Rights Covenants. (No figure indicates no minimum wage).

The UN Convention on the Rights of the Child
Adopted by the General Assembly of the United Nations on 20 November 1989

Text	*Unofficial summary of main provisions*

PREAMBLE

The States Parties to the present Convention.

Considering that in accordance with the principles proclaimed in the Charter of the United Nations, recognition of the inherent dignity and of the equal and inalienable rights of all members of the human family is the foundation of freedom, justice and peace in the world,

Bearing in mind that the peoples of the United Nations have, in the Charter, reaffirmed their faith in fundamental human rights and in the dignity and worth of the human person, and have determined to promote progress and better standards of life in larger freedom,

Recognizing that the United Nations has, in the Universal Declaration of Human Rights and in the International Covenants on Human Rights, proclaimed and agreed that everyone is entitled to all the rights and freedoms set forth therein, without distinction of any kind, such as race, colour, sex, language, religion, political or other opinion, national or social origin, property, birth or other status,

Recalling that, in the Universal Declaration of Human Rights, the United Nations has proclaimed that childhood is entitled to special care and assistance,

Convinced that the family, as the fundamental group of society and the natural environment for the growth and well-being of all its members and particularly children, should be afforded the necessary protection and assistance so that it can fully assume its responsibilities within the community,

Recognizing that the child, for the full and harmonious development of his or her personality, should grow up in a family environment, in an atmosphere of happiness, love and understanding,

Considering that the child should be fully prepared to live an individual life in society, and brought up in the spirit of the ideals proclaimed in the Charter of the United Nations, and in particular in the spirit of peace, dignity, tolerance, freedom, equality and solidarity,

PREAMBLE

The preamble: recalls the basic principles of the United Nations and specific provisions of certain relevant human rights treaties and proclamations; reaffirms the fact that children, because of their vulnerability, need special care and protection; and places special emphasis on the primary caring and protective responsibility of the family, the need for legal and other protection of the child before and after birth, the importance of respect for the cultural values of the child's community, and the vital role of international cooperation in achieving the realization of children's rights.

Text

Bearing in mind that the need for extending particular care to the child has been stated in the Geneva Declaration on the Rights of the Child of 1924 and in the Declaration of the Rights of the Child adopted by the United Nations in 1959 and recognized in the Universal Declaration of Human Rights, in the International Covenant on Civil and Political Rights (in particular in articles 23 and 24), in the International Covenant on Economic, Social and Cultural Rights (in particular in its article 10) and in the statutes and relevant instruments of specialized agencies and international organizations concerned with the welfare of children,

Bearing in mind that, as indicated in the Declaration of the Rights of the Child adopted by the General Assembly of the United Nations on 20 November 1959, 'the child, by reason of his physical and mental immaturity, needs special safeguards and care, including appropriate legal protection, before as well as after birth,'

Recalling the provisions of the Declaration on Social and Legal Principles relating to the Protection and Welfare of Children, with Special Reference to Foster Placement and Adoption Nationally and Internationally (General Assembly Resolution 41/85 of 3 December 1986); the United Nations Standard Minimum Rules for the Administration of Juvenile Justice ('The Beijing Rules') (General Assembly Resolution 40/33 of 29 November 1985); and the Declaration on the Protection of Women and Children in Emergency and Armed Conflict (General Assembly Resolution 3318 (XXIX) of 14 December 1974),

Recognizing that in all countries in the world there are children living in exceptionally difficult conditions, and that such children need special consideration,

Taking due account of the importance of the traditions and cultural values of each people for the protection and harmonious development of the child,

Recognizing the importance of international cooperation for improving the living conditions of children in every country, in particular in the developing countries,

Have agreed as follows:

PART I

Article 1

Definition of a child

For the purposes of the present Convention a child means every human being below the age of 18 years unless, under the law applicable to the child, majority is attained earlier.

All persons under 18, unless by law majority is attained at an earlier age.

Text	*Unofficial summary of main provisions*

Article 2

1. The States Parties to the present Convention shall respect and ensure the rights set forth in this Convention to each child within their jurisdiction without discrimination of any kind, colour, sex, language, religion, political or other opinion, national, ethnic or social origin, property, disability, birth or other status.

2. States Parties shall take all appropriate measures to ensure that the child is protected against all forms of discrimination or punishment on the basis of the status, activities, expressed opinions, or beliefs of the child's parents, legal guardians, or family members.

Non-discrimination

The principle that all rights apply to all children without exception, and the State's obligation to protect children from any form of discrimination. The State must not violate any right, and must take positive action to promote them all.

Article 3

1. In all actions concerning children, whether undertaken by public or private social welfare institutions, courts of law, administrative authorities or legislative bodies, the best interests of the child shall be a primary consideration.

2. States Parties undertake to ensure the child such protection and care as is necessary for his or her well-being, taking into account the rights and duties of his or her parents, legal guardians, or other individuals legally responsible for him or her, and, to this end, shall take all appropriate legislative and administrative measures.

3. States Parties shall ensure that the institutions, services and facilities responsible for the care or protection of children shall conform with the standards established by competent authorities, particularly in the areas of safety, health, in the number and suitability of their staff as well as competent supervision.

Best interests of the child

All actions concerning the child should take full account of his or her best interests. The State is to provide adequate care when parents or others responsible fail to do so.

Article 4

States Parties shall undertake all appropriate legislative, administrative, and other measures, for the implementation of the rights recognized in the Convention. In regard to economic, social and cultural rights, States Parties shall undertake such measures to the maximum extent of their available resources and, where needed, within the framework of international co-operation.

Implementation of rights

The State's obligation to translate the rights in the convention into reality.

Article 5

States Parties shall respect the responsibilities, rights, and duties of parents or, where applicable, the members of the extended family or community as provided for by the local custom, legal guardians or other persons legally responsible for the child, to provide, in a manner consistent with the evolving capacities of the child, appropriate direction and guidance in the exercise by the child of the rights recognized in the present Convention.

Parental guidance and the child's evolving capacities

The State's duty to respect the rights and responsibilities of parents and the wider family to provide guidance appropriate to the child's evolving capacities.

Text	*Unofficial summary of main provisions*

Article 6

1. States Parties recognize that every child has the inherent right to life.

2. States Parties shall ensure to the maximum extent possible the survival and development of the child.

Survival and development

The inherent right to life, and the State's obligation to ensure the child's survival and development.

Article 7

1. The child shall be registered immediately after birth and shall have the right from birth to a name, the right to acquire a nationality, and, as far as possible, the right to know and be cared for by his or her parents.

2. States Parties shall ensure the implementation of these rights in accordance with their national law and their obligations under the relevant international instruments in this field, in particular where the child would otherwise be stateless.

Name and nationality

The right to have a name from birth and to be granted a nationality.

Article 8

1. States Parties undertake to respect the right of the child to preserve his or her identity, including nationality, name and family relations as recognized by law without unlawful interference.

2. Where a child is illegally deprived of some or all of the elements of his or her identity, States Parties shall provide appropriate assistance and protection, with a view to speedily re-establishing his or her identity.

Preservation of identity

The State's obligation to protect and, if necessary, re-establish the basic aspects of a child's identity (name, nationality and family ties).

Article 9

1. States Parties shall ensure that a child shall not be separated from his or her parents against their will, except when competent authorities subject to judicial review determine, in accordance with applicable law and procedures, that such separation is necessary for the best interests of the child. Such determination may be necessary in a particular case such as one involving abuse or neglect of the child by the parents, or one where the parents are living separately and a decision must be made at to the child's place of residence.

2. In any proceedings pursuant to paragraph 1, all interested parties shall be given an opportunity to participate in the proceedings and make their views known.

3. States Parties shall respect the right of the child who is separated from one or both parents to maintain personal relations and direct contact with both parents on a regular basis, except if it is contrary to the child's best interests.

Separation from parents

The child's right to live with his/her parents unless this is deemed incompatible with his/her best interests; the right to maintain contact with both parents if separated from one or both; the duties of States in cases where such separation results from State action.

Text

*Unofficial summary
of main provisions*

4. Where such separation results from any action initiated by a State Party, such as the detention, imprisonment, exile, deportation or death (including death arising from any cause while the person is in the custody of the State) of one or both parents or of the child, that State Party shall, upon request, provide the parents, the child or, if appropriate, another member of the family with the essential information concerning the whereabouts of the absent member(s) of the family unless the provision of the information would be detrimental to the well-being of the child. States Parties shall further ensure that the submission of such a request shall of itself entail no adverse consequences for the person(s) concerned.

Article 10

1. In accordance with the obligation of States Parties under article 9, paragraph 1, applications by a child or his or her parents to enter or leave a State Party for the purpose of family reunification shall be dealt with by States Parties in a positive, humane and expeditious manner. States Parties shall further ensure that the submission of such a request shall entail no adverse consequences for the applicants and for the members of their family.

2. A child whose parents reside in different States shall have the right to maintain on a regular basis save in exceptional circumstances personal relations and direct contacts with both parents. Towards that end and in accordance with the obligation of States Parties under article 9, paragraph 2, States Parties shall respect the right of the child and his or her parents to leave any country, including their own, and to enter their own country. The right to leave any country shall be subject only to such restrictions as are prescribed by law and which are necessary to protect the national security, public order (*ordre public*), public health or morals or the rights and freedoms of others and are consistent with the other rights recognized in the present Convention.

Article 11

1. States Parties shall take measures to combat the illicit transfer and non-return of children abroad.

2. To this end, States Parties shall promote the conclusion of bilateral or multilateral agreements or accession to existing agreements.

Family reunification

The right of children and their parents to leave any country and to enter their own in order to be reunited or to maintain the child–parent relationship.

Illicit transfer and non-return

The State's obligation to try to prevent and remedy the kidnapping or retention of children abroad by a parent or third party.

Text

Unofficial summary
of main provisions

Article 12

1. States Parties shall assure to the child who is capable of forming his or her own views the right to express those views freely in all matters affecting the child, the views of the child being given due weight in accordance with the age and maturity of the child.

2. For this purpose, the child shall in particular be provided the opportunity to be heard in any judicial and administrative proceedings affecting the child, either directly, or through a representative or an appropriate body, in a manner consistent with the procedural rules of national law.

The child's opinion

The child's right to express an opinion, and to have that opinion taken into account, in any matter or procedure affecting the child.

Article 13

1. The child shall have the right to freedom of expression; this right shall include freedom to seek, receive and impart information and ideas of all kinds, regardless of frontiers, either orally, in writing or in print, in the form of art, or through any other media of the child's choice.

2. The exercise of this right may be subject to certain restrictions, but these shall only be such as are provided by law and are necessary:

(a) for respect of the rights or reputations of others; or

(b) for the protection of national security or of public order (*ordre public*), or of public health or morals.

Freedom of expression

The child's right to obtain and make known information, and to express his or her views, unless this would violate the rights of others.

Article 14

1. States Parties shall respect the right of the child to freedom of thought, conscience and religion.

2. States Parties shall respect the rights and duties of the parents and, when applicable, legal guardians to provide direction to the child in the exercise of his or her right in a manner consistent with the evolving capacities of the child.

3. Freedom to manifest one's religion or beliefs may be subject only to such limitations as are prescribed by law and are necessary to protect public safety, order, health, or morals or the fundamental rights and freedoms of others.

Freedom of thought, conscience and religion

The child's right to freedom of thought, conscience and religion, subject to appropriate parental guidance and national law.

Article 15

1. States Parties recognize the rights of the child to freedom of association and to freedom of peaceful assembly.

2. No restrictions may be placed on the exercise of these rights other than those imposed in conformity with the law and which are necessary in a democratic society in the interests of national security or public safety, public order (*ordre public*), the protection of public mental health or morals or the protection of the rights and freedoms of others.

Freedom of association

The right of children to meet with others and to join or set up associations, unless the fact of doing so violates the rights of others.

Text

*Unofficial summary
of main provisions*

Article 16

1. No child shall be subjected to arbitrary or unlawful interference with his or her privacy, family, home or correspondence, nor to unlawful attacks on his or her honour and reputation.

2. The child has the right to the protection of the law against such interference or attacks.

Protection of privacy

The right to protection from interference with privacy, family, home and correspondence, and from libel or slander.

Article 17

States Parties recognize the important function performed by the mass media and shall ensure that the child has access to information and material from a diversity of national and international sources, especially those aimed at the promotion of his or her social, spiritual and moral well-being and physical and mental health. To this end, States Parties shall:

(a) Encourage the mass media to disseminate information and material of social and cultural benefit to the child and in accordance with the spirit of article 29;

(b) Encourage international co-operation in the production, exchange and dissemination of such information and material from a diversity of cultural, national and international sources;

(c) Encourage the production and dissemination of children's books;

(d) Encourage the mass media to have particular regard to the linguistic needs of the child who belongs to a minority group or who is indigenous;

(e) Encourage the development of appropriate guidelines for the protection of the child from information and material injurious to his or her well-being bearing in mind the provisions of articles 13 and 18.

Access to appropriate information

The role of the media is disseminating information to children that is consistent with moral well-being and knowledge and understanding among peoples, and respects the child's cultural background. The State is to take measures to encourage this and to protect children from harmful materials.

Article 18

1. States Parties shall use their best efforts to ensure recognition of the principle that both parents have common responsibilities for the upbringing and development of the child. Parents or, as the case may be, legal guardians, have the primary responsibility for the upbringing and development of the child. The best interests of the child will be their basic concern.

2. For the purpose of guaranteeing and promoting the rights set forth in this Convention, States Parties shall render appropriate assistance to parents and legal guardians in the performance of their child-rearing responsibilities and shall ensure the development of institutions, facilities and services for the care of children.

Parental responsibilities

The principle that both parents have joint primary responsibility for bringing up their children, and that the State should support them in this task.

Text	*Unofficial summary of main provisions*

3. States Parties shall take all appropriate measures to ensure that children of working parents have the right to benefit from child care services and facilities for which they are eligible.

Article 19

Protection from abuse and neglect

1. States Parties shall take all appropriate legislative, administrative, social and educational measures to protect the child from all forms of physical or mental violence, injury or abuse, neglect or negligent treatment, maltreatment or exploitation including sexual abuse, while in the care of parent(s), legal guardian(s) or any other person who has the care of the child.

The State's obligation to protect children from all forms of maltreatment perpetrated by parents or others responsible for their care, and to undertake preventive and treatment programmes in this regard.

2. Such protective measures should, as appropriate, include effective procedures for the establishment of social programmes to provide necessary support for the child and for those who have the care of the child, as well as for other forms of prevention and for identification, reporting, referral, investigation, treatment, and follow-up of instances of child maltreatment described heretofore, and, as appropriate, for judicial involvement.

Article 20

Protection of children without families

1. A child temporarily or permanently deprived of his or her family environment, or in whose own best interests cannot be allowed to remain in that environment, shall be entitled to special protection and assistance provided by the State.

The State's obligation to provide special protection for children deprived of their family environment and to ensure that appropriate alternative family care or institutional placement is made available to them, taking into account the child's cultural background.

2. States Parties shall in accordance with their national laws ensure alternative care for such a child.

3. Such care could include, *inter alia*, foster placement, Kafala of Islamic law, adoption, or if necessary placement in suitable institutions for the care of children. When considering solutions, due regard shall be paid to the desirability of continuity in a child's upbringing and to the child's ethnic, religious, cultural and linguistic background.

Article 21

Adoption

States Parties which recognize and/or permit the system of adoption shall ensure that the best interests of the child shall be the paramount consideration and they shall:

In countries where adoption is recognition and/or allowed, it shall only be carried out in the best interests of the child, with all necessary safeguards for a given child and authorization by the competent authorities.

(a) ensure that the adoption of a child is authorized only by competent authorities who determine, in accordance with applicable law and procedures and on the basis of all pertinent and reliable information, that the adoption is permissible in view of the child's status concerning parents, relatives and legal guardians and that, if required, the persons concerned have given their informed consent to the adoption on the basis of such counselling as may be necessary;

Text

Unofficial summary of main provisions

(b) recognize that intercounty adoption may be considered as an alternative means of child's care, if the child cannot be placed in a foster or an adoptive family or cannot in any suitable manner be cared for in the child's country of origin;

(c) ensure that the child concerned by intercountry adoption enjoys safeguards and standards equivalent to those existing in the case of national adoption;

(d) take all appropriate measures to ensure that, in intercountry adoption, the placement does not result in improper financial gain for those involved in it;

(e) promote, where appropriate, the objectives of this article by concluding bilateral or multilateral arrangements or agreements, and endeavour, within this framework, to ensure that the placement of the child in another country is carried out by competent authorities or organs.

Article 22

Refugee children

1. States Parties shall take appropriate measures to ensure that a child who is seeking refugee status or who is considered a refugee in accordance with applicable international or domestic law and procedures shall, whether unaccompanied or accompanied by his or her parents or by any other person, receive appropriate protection and humanitarian assistance in the enjoyment of applicable rights set forth in this Convention and in other international human rights or humanitarian instruments to which the said States are Parties.

Special protection to be granted to children who are refugees or seeking refugee status, and the State's obligation to cooperate with competent organizations providing such protection and assistance.

2. For this purpose, States Parties shall provide, as they consider appropriate, cooperation in any efforts by the United Nations and other competent intergovernmental organizations or non-governmental organizations co-operating with the United Nations to protect and assist such a child and to trace the parents or other members of the family of any refugee child in order to obtain information necessary for reunification with his or her family. In cases where no parents or other members of the family can be found, the child shall be accorded the same protection as any other child permanently or temporarily deprived of his or her family environment for any reason, as set forth in the present Convention.

Article 23

Handicapped children

1. States Parties recognize that a mentally or physically disabled child should enjoy a full and decent life, in conditions which ensure dignity, promote self-reliance, and facilitate the child's active participation in the community.

The right of handicapped children to special care, education and training designed to help them to achieve greatest possible self-reliance and to lead a full and active life in society.

2. States Parties recognize the right of the disabled child to special care and shall encourage and ensure the extension, subject to available resources, to the eligible child and those responsible for his or her care, of assistance for which application is made and which is appropriate to the child's condition and to the circumstances of the parents or others caring for the child.

Text

Unofficial summary of main provisions

3. Recognizing the special needs of a disabled child, assistance extended in accordance with paragraph 2 shall be provided free of charge, whenever possible, taking into account the financial resources of the parents or others caring for the child, and shall be designed to ensure that the disabled child has effective access to and receives education, training, health care services, rehabilitation services, preparation for employment and recreation opportunities in a manner conducive to the child's achieving the fullest possible social integration and individual development, including his or her cultural and spiritual development.

4. States Parties shall promote in the spirit of international co-operation the exchange of appropriate information in the field of preventive health care and of medical, psychological and functional treatment of disabled children, including dissemination of and access to information concerning methods of rehabilitation education and vocational services, with the aim of enabling States Parties to improve their capabilities and skills and to widen their experience in these areas. In this regard, particular account shall be taken of the needs of developing countries.

Article 24

1. States Parties recognize the right of the child to the enjoyment of the highest attainable standard of health and to facilities for the treatment of illness and rehabilitation of health. States Parties shall strive to ensure that no child is deprived of his or her right to access to such health care services.

2. States Parties shall pursue full implementation of this right and, in particular, shall taken appropriate measures:

(a) to diminish infant and child mortality,

(b) to ensure the provision of necessary medical assistance and health care to all children with emphasis on the development of primary health care,

(c) to combat disease and malnutrition including within the framework of primary health care, through inter alia the application of readily available technology and through the provision of adequate nutritious foods and clean drinking water, taking into consideration the dangers and risks of environmental pollution,

(d) to ensure appropriate pre- and post-natal health care for mothers,

(e) to ensure that all segments of society, in particular parents and children, are informed, have access to education and are supported in the use of, basic knowledge of child health and nutrition, the advantages of breast-feeding, hygiene and environmental sanitation and the prevention of accidents.

(f) to develop preventive health care, guidance for parents, and family planning education and services.

Health and health services

The right to the highest level of health possible and to access to health and medical services, with special emphasis on primary and preventive health care, public health education and the diminution of infant mortality. The State's obligation to work towards the abolition of harmful traditional practices. Emphasis is laid on the need for international cooperation to ensure this right.

Text	*Unofficial summary of main provisions*

3. States Parties shall take all effective and appropriate measures with a view to abolishing traditional practices prejudicial to the health of children.

4. States Parties undertake to promote and encourage international co-operation with a view to achieving progressively the full realization of the right recognized in this article. In this regard, particular account shall be taken of the needs of developing countries.

Article 25

States Parties recognize the right of a child who has been placed by the competent authorities for the purposes of care, protection, or treatment of his or her physical or mental health, to a periodic review of the treatment provided to the child and all other circumstances relevant to his or her placement.

Periodic review of placement

The right of children placed by the State for reasons of care, protection or treatment to have all aspects of that placement evaluated regularly.

Article 26

1. States Parties shall recognize for every child the right to benefit from social security, including social insurance, and shall take the necessary measures to achieve the full realization of this right in accordance with their national law.

2. The benefits should, where appropriate, be granted taking into account the resources and the circumstances of the child and persons having responsibility for the maintenance of the child as well as any other consideration relevant to an application for benefits made by or on behalf of the child.

Social security

The right of children to benefit from social security.

Article 27

1. States Parties recognize the right of every child to a standard of living adequate for the child's physical, mental, spiritual, moral and social development.

2. The parent(s) or others responsible for the child have the primary responsibility to secure, within their abilities and financial capacities, the conditions of living necessary for the child's development.

3. States Parties in accordance with national conditions and within their means shall take appropriate measures to assist parents and others responsible for the child to implement this right and shall in case of need provide material assistance and support programmes, particularly with regard to nutrition, clothing and housing.

4. States Parties shall take all appropriate measures to secure the recovery of maintenance for the child from the parents or other persons having financial responsibility for the child, both within the State Party and from abroad. In particular, where the person having financial responsibility for the child lives in a State different from that of the child, States Parties shall promote the accession to international agreements or the conclusion of such agreements, as well as the making of other appropriate arrangements.

Standard of living

The right of children to benefit from an adequate standard of living, the primary responsibility of parents of provide this, and the State's duty to ensure that this responsibility is first fulfillable and then fulfilled, where necessary through the recovery of maintenance.

Text	*Unofficial summary of main provisions*

Article 28

1. States Parties recognize the right of the child to education, and with a view to achieving this right progressively and on the basis of equal opportunity, they shall, in particular:

(a) make primary education compulsory and available free to all;

(b) encourage the development of different forms of secondary education, including general and vocational education, make them available and accessible to every child, and take appropriate measures such as the introduction of free education and offering financial assistance in case of need;

(c) make higher education accessible to all on the basis of capacity by every appropriate means;

(d) make educational and vocational information and guidance available and accessible to all children;

(e) take measures to encourage regular attendance at schools and the reduction of drop-out rates;

2. States Parties shall take all appropriate measures to ensure that school discipline is administered in a manner consistent with the child's human dignity and in conformity with the present Convention.

3. States Parties shall promote and encourage international co-operation in matters relating to education, in particular with a view to contributing to the elimination of ignorance and illiteracy throughout the world and facilitating access to scientific and technical knowledge and modern teaching methods. In this regard, particular account shall be taken of the needs of developing countries.

Education

The child's right to education, and the State's duty to ensure that primary education at least is made free and compulsory. Administration of school discipline is to reflect the child's human dignity. Emphasis is laid on the need for international cooperation to ensure this right.

Article 29

1. States Parties agree that the education of the child shall be directed to:

(a) the development of the child's personality, talents and mental and physical abilities to their fullest potential;

(b) the development of respect for human rights and fundamental freedoms, and for the principles enshrined in the Charter of the United Nations;

(c) the development of respect for the child's parents, his or her own cultural identity, language and values, for the national values of the country in which the child is living, the country from which he or she may originate, and for civilizations different from his or her own;

(d) the preparation of the child for responsible life in a free society, in the spirit of understanding, peace, tolerance, equality of sexes, and friendship among all peoples, ethnic, national and religious groups and persons of indigenous origin;

(e) the development of respect for the natural environment.

Aims of Education

The State's recognition that education should be directed at developing the child's personality and talents, preparing the child for active life as an adult, fostering respect for basic human rights and developing respect for the child's own cultural and national values and those of others.

Text

Unofficial summary of main provisions

2. No part of this article or article 28 shall be construed so as to interfere with the liberty of individuals and bodies to establish and direct educational institutions, subject always to the observance of the principles set forth in paragraph 1 of this article and to the requirements tat the education given in such institutions shall conform to such minimum standards as may be laid down by the State.

Article 30

In those States in which ethnic, religious or linguistic minorities or persons of indigenous origin exist, a child belonging to such a minority or who is indigenous shall not be denied the right, in community with other members of his or her group, to enjoy his or her own culture, to profess and practice his or her own religion, or to use his or her own language.

Children of minorities or indigenous populations

The right of the children of minority communities and indigenous populations to enjoy their own culture and to practice their own religion and language.

Article 31

1. States Parties recognize the right of the child to rest and leisure, to engage in play and recreational activities appropriate to the age of the child and to participate freely in cultural life and the arts.

2. States Parties shall respect and promote the right of the child to fully participate in cultural and artistic life and shall encourage the provision of appropriate and equal opportunities for cultural, artistic, recreational and leisure activity.

Leisure, recreation and cultural activities

The right of children to leisure, play and participation in cultural and artistic activities.

Article 32

1. States Parties recognize the right of the child to be protected from economic exploitation and from performing any work that is likely to be hazardous or to interfere with the child's education, or to be harmful to the child's health or physical, mental, spiritual, moral or social development.

2. States Parties shall take legislative, administrative, social and educational measures to ensure the implementation of this article. To this end, and having regard to the relevant provisions of other international instruments, States Parties shall in particular:

(a) provide for a minimum age or minimum ages for admissions to employment;

(b) provide for appropriate regulations of the hours and conditions of employment; and

(c) provide for appropriate penalties or other sanctions to ensure the effective enforcement of this article.

Child labour

The State's obligation to protect children from engaging in work that constitutes a threat to their health, education or development, to set minimum ages for employment, and to regulate conditions of employment.

Text

*Unofficial summary
of main provisions*

Article 33

States Parties shall take all appropriate measures, including legislative, administrative, social and educational measures, to protect children from the illicit use of narcotic drugs and psychotropic substances as defined in the relevant international treaties, and to prevent the use of children in the illicit production and trafficking of such substances.

Drug abuse

The child's right to protection from the use of narcotic and psychotropic drugs and from being involved in their production or distribution.

Article 34

State Parties undertake to protect the child from all forms of sexual exploitation and sexual abuse. For these purposes States Parties shall in particular take all appropriate national, bilateral and multilateral measures to prevent:

(a) the inducement or coercion of a child to engage in any unlawful sexual activity;

(b) the exploitative use of children in prostitution of other unlawful sexual practices;

(c) the exploitative use of children in pornographic performances and materials.

Sexual exploitation

The child's right to protection from sexual exploitation and abuse, including prostitution and involvement in pornography.

Article 35

States Parties shall take all appropriate national, bilateral and multilateral measures to prevent the abduction, the sale of or traffic in children for any purpose or in any form.

Sale, trafficking and abduction

The State's obligation to make every effort to prevent the sale, trafficking and abduction of children.

Article 36

States Parties shall protect the child against all other forms of exploitation prejudicial to any aspects of the child's welfare.

Other forms of exploitation

The child's right to protection from all other forms of exploitation not covered in articles 32, 33, 34 and

Article 37

States Parties shall ensure that:

(a) No child shall be subjected to torture or other cruel, inhuman or degrading treatment or punishment. Neither capital punishment nor life imprisonment without possibility of release shall be imposed for offences committed by persons below 18 years of age;

(b) No child shall be deprived of his or her liberty unlawfully or arbitrarily. The arrest, detention or imprisonment of a child shall be in conformity with the law and shall be used only as a measure of last resort and for the shortest appropriate period of time;

Torture and deprivation of liberty

The prohibition of torture, cruel treatment or punishment, capital punishment, life imprisonment, and unlawful arrest or deprivation of liberty. The principles of appropriate treatment, separation from detained adults, contact with family and access to legal and other assistance.

Text	*Unofficial summary of main provisions*

(c) Every child deprived of liberty shall be treated with humanity and respect for the inherent dignity of the human person, and in a manner which takes into account the needs of persons of their age. In particular every child deprived of liberty shall be separated from adults unless it is considered in the child's best interest not to do so and shall have the right to maintain contact with his or her family through correspondence and visits, save in exceptional circumstances.

(d) Every child deprived of his or her liberty shall have the right to prompt access to legal and other appropriate assistance as well as the right to challenge the legality of the deprivation of his or her liberty before a court or other competent, independent and impartial authority and to a prompt decision on any such action.

Article 38

1. State Parties undertake to respect and to ensure respect for rules of international humanitarian law applicable to them in armed conflicts which are relevant to the child.

2. State Parties shall take all feasible measures to ensure that persons who have not attained the age of 15 years do not take a direct part in hostilities.

3. State Parties shall refrain from recruiting any person who has not attained the age of 15 years into their armed forces. In recruiting among those persons who have attained the age of 15 years but who have not attained the age of 18 years, States Parties shall endeavour to give priority to those who are oldest.

4. In accordance with their obligations under international humanitarian law to protect the civilian population in armed conflicts, States Parties shall take all feasible measures to ensure protection and care of children who are affected by an armed conflict.

Armed conflicts

The obligation of States to respect and ensure respect for humanitarian law as it applies to children. The principle that no child under 15 take a direct part in hostilities or be recruited into the armed forces, and that all children affected by armed conflict benefit from protection and care.

Article 39

States Parties shall take all appropriate measures to promote physical and psychological recovery and social re-integration of a child victim of: any form of neglect, exploitation, or abuse; torture or any other form of cruel, inhuman or degrading treatment or punishment; or armed conflicts. Such recovery and re-integration shall take place in an environment which fosters the health, self-respect and dignity of the child.

Rehabilitative care

The State's obligation to ensure that child victims of armed conflicts, torture, neglect, maltreatment or exploitation receive appropriate treatment for their recovery and social re-integration.

Text

Article 40

1. States Parties recognize the right of every child alleged as, accused of, or recognized as having infringed the penal law to be treated in a manner consistent with the promotion of the child's sense of dignity and worth, which reinforces the child's respect for the human rights and fundamental freedoms of others and which takes into account the child's age and the desirability of promoting the child's re-integration and the child's assuming a constructive role in society.

2. To this end, and having regard to the relevant provisions of international instruments, States Parties shall, in particular, ensure that:

(a) No child shall be alleged as, be accused of, or recognized as having infringed the penal law by reason of acts or omissions which were not prohibited by national or international law at the time they were committed;

(b) Every child alleged as or accused of having infringed the penal law has at least the following guarantees:

  (i) to be presumed innocent until proven guilty according to law;

  (ii) to be informed promptly and directly of the charges against him or her, and if appropriate through his or her parents or legal guardian, and to have legal or other appropriate assistance in the preparation and presentation of his or her defence;

  (iii) to have the matter determined without delay by a competent, independent and impartial authority or judicial body in a fair hearing according to law, in the presence of legal or other appropriate assistance and, unless it is considered not to be in the best interest of the child, in particular, taking into account his or her age or situation, his or her parents or legal guardians.

  (iv) not to be compelled to give testimony of to confess guilt; to examine or have examined adverse witnesses and to obtain the participation and examination of witnesses on his or her behalf under conditions of equality;

  (v) if considered to have infringed the penal law, to have this decision and any measures imposed in consequence thereof reviewed by a higher competent, independent and impartial authority or judicial body according to law;

  (vi) to have the free assistance of an interpreter if the child cannot understand or speak the language used;

  (vii) to have his or her privacy fully respected at all stages of the proceedings.

Administration of juvenile justice

The right of the children alleged or recognized as having committed an offence to respect for their human rights and, in particular, to benefit from all aspects of the due process of law, including legal or other assistance in preparing and presenting their defence. The principle that recourse to judicial proceedings and institutional placements should be avoided wherever possible and appropriate.

Text	*Unofficial summary of main provisions*

3. States Parties shall seek to promote the establishment of laws, procedures, authorities and institutions specifically applicable to children alleged as, accused of, or recognized as having infringed the penal law, and in particular:

(a) the establishment of a minimum age below which children shall be presumed not to have the capacity to infringe the penal law;

(b) whenever appropriate and desirable, measures for dealing with such children without resorting to judicial proceedings, providing that human rights and legal safeguards are fully respected.

4. A variety of dispositions, such as care, guidance and supervision orders; counselling; probation; foster care; education and vocational training programmes and other alternatives to institutional care shall be available to ensure that children are dealt with in a manner appropriate to their well-being and proportionate both to their circumstances and the offence.

Article 41

Nothing in this Convention shall affect any provisions that are more conducive to the realization of the rights of the child and that may be contained in:

(a) the law of a State Party

(b) international law in force for that State.

Respect for existing standards

The principle that, if any standards set in national law or other applicable international instruments are higher than those of this Convention, it is the higher standard that applies.

PART II
Article 42

States Parties undertake to make the principles and provisions of the Convention widely known, by appropriate and active means, to adults and children alike.

Article 43

1. For the purposes of examining the progress made by States Parties in achieving the realization of the obligations undertaken in the present Convention, there shall be established a Committee on the Rights of the Child, which shall carry out the functions hereinafter provided.

2. The Committee shall consist of 10 experts of high moral standing and recognized competence in the field covered by this Convention. The members of the Committee shall be elected by States Parties from among their nationals and shall serve in their personal capacity, consideration being given to equitable geographical distribution as well as to the principal legal system.

Implementation and entry into force

The provisions of articles 42–54 notably foresee:

(i) the State's obligation to make the rights contained in this Convention widely known to both adults and children.

(ii) the setting up of a Committee on the Rights of the child composed of ten experts, which will consider reports that States Parties to the Convention are to submit two years after ratification and every five years thereafter. The Convention enters into force – and the Committee would therefore be set up – once 20 countries have ratified it.

(iii) States Parties are to make their reports widely available to the general public.

Text

3. The members of the Committee shall be elected by secret ballot from a list of persons nominated by States Parties. Each State Party may nominate one person from among its own nationals.

4. The initial election to the Committee shall be held no later than six months after the date of the entry into force of the present Convention and thereafter every second year. At least four months before the date of each election, the Secretary General of the United Nations shall address a letter to States Parties inviting them to submit their nominations within two months. The Secretary-General shall subsequently prepare a list in alphabetical order of all persons thus nominated, indicating States Parties which have nominated them, and shall submit it to the States Parties to the present Convention.

5. The elections shall be held at meetings of States Parties convened by the Secretary-General at United Nations Headquarters. At those meetings, for which two-thirds of States Parties shall constitute a quorum, the persons elected to the Committee shall be those who obtain the largest number of votes and an absolute majority of the votes of the representatives of States Parties present and voting.

6. The members of the Committee shall be elected for a term of four years. They shall be eligible for re-election if renominated. The term of five of the members elected at the first election shall expire at the end of two years; immediately after the first election the names of these five members shall be chosen by lot by the Chairman of the meeting.

7. If a member of the Committee dies or resigns or declares that for any other cause he or she can no longer perform the duties of the Committee, the State Party which nominated the member shall appoint another expert from among its nationals to serve for the remainder of the term, subject to the approval of the Committee.

8. The Committee shall establish its own rules of procedure.

9. The Committee shall elects its officers for a period of two years.

10. The meetings of the Committee shall normally be held at the United Nations Headquarters or at any other convenient place as determined by the Committee. The Committee shall normally meet annually. The duration of the meetings of the Committee shall be determined, and reviewed, if necessary, by a meeting of the States Parties to the present Convention, subject to the approval of the General Assembly.

11. The Secretary-General of the United Nations shall provide the necessary staff and facilities for the effective performance of the functions of the Committee under the present Convention.

Unofficial summary of main provisions

(iv) The Committee may propose that special studies be undertaken on specific issues relating to the rights of the child, and may make its evaluations known to each State Party concerned as well as to the UN General Assembly.

(v) in order to foster the effective implementation of the Convention and to encourage international cooperation; the specialized agencies of the UN (such as the ILO, WHO and UNESCO) and UNICEF would be able to attend the meetings of the Committee. Together with any other body recognized as 'competent', including NGOs in consultative status with the UN and UN organs such as the UNHCR, they can submit pertinent information to the Committee and be asked to advise on the optimal implementation of the Convention.

Text

12. With the approval of the General Assembly, the members of the Committee established under the present Convention shall receive emoluments from the United Nations resources on such terms and conditions as the Assembly may decide.

Article 44

1. States Parties undertake to submit to the Committee, through the Secretary-General of the United Nations, reports on the measures they have adopted which give effect to the rights recognized herein and on the progress made on the enjoyment of those rights:

(a) within two years of the entry into force of the Convention for the State Party concerned,

(b) thereafter every five years.

2. Reports made under this article shall indicate factors and difficulties, if any, affecting the degree of fulfilment of the obligations under the present Convention. Reports shall also contain sufficient information to provide the Committee with a comprehensive understanding of the implementation of the Convention in the country concerned.

3. A State Party which has submitted a comprehensive initial report to the Committee need not in its subsequent reports submitted in accordance with paragraph 1(b) repeat basic information previously provided.

4. The Committee may request from States Parties further information relevant to the implementation of the Convention.

5. The Committee shall submit to the General Assembly of the United Nations through the Economic and Social Council, every two years, reports on its activities.

6. States Parties shall make their reports widely available to the pubic in their own countries.

Article 45

In order to foster the effective implementation of the Convention and to encourage international co-operation in the field covered by the Convention:

(a) The specialized agencies, UNICEF and other United Nations organs shall be entitled to be represented at the consideration of the implementation of such provisions of the present Convention a fall within the scope of their mandate. The Committee may invite the specialized agencies, UNICEF and other competent bodies as it may consider appropriate to provide expert advice on the implementation of the Convention in areas within the scope of their respective mandates. The Committee may invite the specialized agencies, UNICEF and other United Nations organs to submit reports on the implementation of the Convention in areas falling within the scope of their activities.

Text

(b) The Committee shall transmit, as it may consider appropriate, to the specialized agencies, UNICEF and other competent bodies, any reports from States Parties that contain a request, or indicate a need, for technical advice or assistance along with the Committee's observations and suggestions, if any, on these requests or indications.

(c) the Committee may recommend to the General Assembly to request the Secretary-General to undertake on its behalf studies on specific issues relating to the rights of the child.

(d) the Committee may make suggestions and general recommendations based on information received pursuant to articles 44 and 45 of this Convention. Such suggestions and general recommendations shall be transmitted to any State Party concerned and reported to the General Assembly, together with comments, if any, from States Parties.

PART III

Article 46

The present Convention shall be open for signature by all States.

Article 47

The present Convention is subject to ratification. Instruments of ratification shall be deposited with the Secretary-General of the United Nations.

Article 48

The present Convention shall remain open for accession by any State. The instruments of accession shall be deposited with the Secretary-General of the United Nations.

Article 49

1. The present Convention shall enter into force on the thirtieth day following the date of deposit with the Secretary-General of the United Nations of the twentieth instrument of ratification or accession.

2. For each State ratifying or acceding to the Convention after the deposit of the twentieth instrument of ratification or accession, the Convention shall enter into force on the thirtieth day after the deposit by such States of its instrument of ratification or accession.

Text

Article 50

1. Any State Party may propose an amendment and file it with the Secretary-General of the United Nations. The Secretary-General shall thereupon communicate the proposed amendments to States Parties with a request that they indicate whether they favour a conference of States Parties for the purpose of considering and voting upon the proposals. In the event that within four months from the date of such communication at least one-third of the States Parties favour such a conference, the Secretary-General shall convene the conference under the auspices of the United Nations. Any amendment adopted by a majority of States Parties present and voting at the conference shall be submitted to the General Assembly of the United Nations for approval.

2. An amendment adopted in accordance with paragraph (1) of this article shall enter into force when it has been approved by the General Assembly of the United Nations and accepted by a two-thirds majority of States Parties.

3. When an amendment enters into force, it shall be binding on those States Parties which have accepted it, other States Parties still being bound by the provisions of this Convention and any earlier amendments which they have accepted.

Article 51

1. The Secretary-General of the United Nations shall receive and circulate to all States the text of reservations made by States at the time of ratification or accession.

2. A reservation incompatible with the object and purpose of the present Convention shall not be permitted.

3. Reservations may be withdrawn at any time by notification to this effect addressed to the Secretary-General of the United Nations who shall then inform all States. Such notification shall take effect on the date on which it is received by the Secretary-General.

Article 52

A State Party may denounce this Convention by written notification to the Secretary-General of the United Nations. Denunciation becomes effective one year after the date of receipt of the notification by the Secretary-General.

Text

Article 53

The Secretary-General of the United Nations is designated as the depositary of the present Convention.

Article 54

The original of the present Convention, of which the Arabic, Chinese, English, French, Russian and Spanish texts are equally authentic, shall be deposited with the Secretary-General of the United Nations.

IN witness thereof the undersigned plenipotentiaries, being duly authorized thereto by their respective governments, have signed the present Convention.

Done at   this   day of   198

Bibliography

Ainsworth, M.D.S. (1979) 'Infant–mother attachment.' *American Psychologist 34,* 932–937.

Alston, P. (1990) *Comments on the Convention.* Paper presented at Global Consultation on Implementation Strategies for Children's Rights, UNICEF/Florence (mimeo).

Alston, P. and Gilmour-Walsh, B. (1996) 'The best interest of the child. Towards a synthesis of children's rights and cultural values.' Paper presented at the International Symposium on the Convention on the Rights of the Child, Salamanca (mimeo).

Andenæs, A. and Haavind, H. (1987) *Små barns vilkår i Norge.* Oslo: Universitetsforlaget.

Andersson, B.-E. (1986) 'Home care or external care? The effects of public child care on children's development when 8 years old.' *Reports from the Department of Education 2.* Stockholm: Stockholm Institute of Education.

Andersson, B.-E. (1990) 'Effects of public day care – a longitudinal study, child development.' Paper presented at ICDC, Florence (mimeo).

Aries, R. (1962) *Centuries of Childhood.* London: Jonathan Cape.

Arnstein, S.R. (1979) 'Eight rungs on the ladder of citizen participation.' *Journal of the American Institute of Planners.*

Baldwin, A. (1968) *Theories of Child Development.* New York: Wiley.

Barneombudet (1987) *Fakta om barn i Norge.* Oslo: Barneombudet.

Barneombudet (1988/89) *Fakta om barn i Norge.* 2. ed. Oslo: Barneombudet.

Barneombudet (1991) *Facts about Children in Norway.* Oslo: Barneombudet.

Baumrind, C. (1971a) 'Current patterns of parental authority.' *Developmental Psychology Monographs 4,* 1, 2.

Baumrind, C. (1971b) 'Harmonius parents and their preschool children.' *Developmental Psychology 4,* 99–102.

Baumrind, D. (1975) 'Early socialization and adolescent competence.' In S.E. Dragastin and G.H. Elder (eds) *Adolescence in the Life Cycle.* Washington DC: Hemisphere Publishing.

Baumrind, D. (1980) 'New directions in socialization research.' *American Psychologist 35,* 639–652.

Bayley, N. (1970) 'Development of mental abilities.' In P.H. Mussen (ed) *Carmichael's Manual of Child Psychology, Vol. 1.* New York: Wiley.

Belsky, J. and Steinberg, L.D. (1978) 'The effects of day care: A critical review.' *Child Development 49*, 929–949.

Borke, H. (1971) 'Interpersonal perception of young children: egocentrism or empathy?' *Developmental Psychology 5.*

Bowlby, J. (1969) *Attachment and Loss, Vol.1: Attachment.* New York: Basic Books.

Bowlby, J. (1973) *Attachment and Loss, Vol.2: Separation, Anxiety, and Anger.* New York: Basic Books.

Bowlby, J. (1980) *Attachment and Loss, Vol. 3: Loss, Sadness and Depression.* New York: Basic Books.

Bråten, S. (1992) 'The virtual other in infants' minds and social feelings.' In A. Heen Wold (ed) *The Dialogigal Alternative.* Oslo: Scandinavia University Press.

Brazelton, T.B. (1982) 'Early intervention: What does it mean?' In H. Fitzgerald, B.M. Lester and M. Yogman. *Theory and Research in Behavioral Pediatrics, Vol. 1.* New York: Plenum.

Brazelton, T.B. (1987) 'Early intervention: What does it mean?' In Gunzenhauser (ed) *Infant Stimulation: For Whom, What Kind, When and How Much?* New Jersey: Johnson and Johnson Pediatric Round Table: 13. Johnson and Johnson Company.

Brazelton, T.B., Koslowski, B. and Main, M. (1974) 'The origin of reciprocity: the early mother–infant interaction.' In M. Lewis and Rosenblum (eds) *The Effects of the Infant on its Caregiver.* New York: John Wiley.

Broughton, J.M. (1981) 'Piaget's structural developmental psychology, III. Function and the problem of knowledge.' *Human Development 24*, 257–285.

Bruner, J. (1983) *Child's Talk.* New York: Norton.

Casas, F. (1994) 'Policies for children in Spain in Council of Europe,' *Evolution of the Role of Children in Family Life: Participation and Negotiation.* Conference proceedings, Ministerio de Asuntos Sociales, Madrid.

Cederblad, M. and Hook, B. (1980) *Daghemsvård for treåringar.* Rapport nr. 121, Stockholm: Laboratoriet før Klinisk Stressforskning, Karolinska Institutet.

Chavez, A. and Martinez, C. (1979) 'Consequences of insufficient nutrition on child character and behaviour.' In D.A. Levitsky (ed) *Malnutrition, Environment, and Behaviour.* New York: Cornell University Press.

Cicirelli, V.G. *et al.* (1969) *The Impact of* Head Start: *An Evaluation of the Effects of* Head Start *on Children's Cognitive and Affective Development.* A report presented to the Office of Economic Opportunity, Ohio State University and Westinghouse Learning Corporation.

Clarke-Stewart, A. (1977) *Child Care in the Family: A Review of Research and Some Propositions for Policy.* New York: Academic.

Clarke-Stewart, K.A. and Fein, G.G. (1983) 'Early childhood programs.' In P.H. Mussen (ed) *Handbook of Child Psychology* (4th ed.) vol.2: Haith, M.M. and Campos, J.J. (eds) *Infancy and Developmental Psychobiology.* New York: Wiley.

Coates, B. and Hartup, W.W. (1969) 'Age and verbalization in observational learning.' *Developmental Psychology 1*, 556–562.

Cohen, C.P. (1990) 'Relationships between the child, the family and the state: the United Nations' Convention on the Rights of the Child.' In M.R. Bayles *et al.* (eds) *Perspectives on the Family.* New York: Edwin Mellen Press.

Cohen, C.P. and Bitensky, S.H. (1996) *Answers to 30 Questions.* New York: Childrights International Research Institute.

Cole, M. and Bruner, J. (1971) 'Cultural differences and inferences about psychological processes.' *American Psychologist 26*, 867–76.

Cole, M. and Scribner, S. (1974) *Culture and Thought: A Psychological Introduction.* New York, Wiley.

Coopersmith, S. (1967) *The Antecedents of Self-Esteem.* San Francisco: Freeman.

Council of Europe (1994) *Evolution of the Role of Children in Family Life: Participation and Negotiation.* Conference proceedings, Ministerio de Asuntos Sociales, Madrid.

De Casper, A.J. and Fifer, W.P. (1982) 'Of human bonding: newborns prefer their mothers' voices.' *Science 208.*

De Casper, A.J. and Spence, M.J. (1986) 'Prenatal maternal speech influences newborns' perception of speech sounds.' *Infant Behaviour and Development 9.*

DeMause, L. (1974) 'The evolution of childhood.' In L. deMause (ed) *The History of Childhood.* New York: Psychohistory Press.

Dennis, W. and Dennis, M.C. (1940) 'The effect of cradling practices upon the onset of walking in Hopi children.' *Journal of Genetic Psychology 56*, 77–86.

Dennis, W. and Sayegh, Y. (1965) 'The effect of supplementary experiences upon behavioral development of infants in institutions.' *Child Development 36*, 81–90.

Detrick, S. (ed) (1992) *The United Nations Convention on the Rights of the Child. A Guide to the 'Travaux Preparatoire'.* Amsterdam: Martinus Nijhoff Publishers.

Dickstein, E.B., Lieber, L.E. and McIntyre, C.W. (1976) 'The development of cognitive, affective and perceptual role-taking skills.' Unpublished paper, quoted in S.G. Moore and D.R. Cooper (eds) (1982) *The Young Child: Reviews of Research Vol.3.* Washington DC: National Association for the Education of Young Children.

Dworkin, G. (1977) *Taking Rights Seriously.* London: Duckworth.

Edgar, D. (1991) *The Development of Competence.* Paper presented at 'Ensuring our Future', CAFHS National Conference, Adelaide, Australia, May 1991.

Eide, A. (1984) 'Barnas rettigheter i menneskerettighetssystemet.' *Mennesker og Rettigheter: Nordic Journal on Human Rights 4*, 2–5.

Erikson, E.H. (1950) *Childhood and Society.* New York: Norton.

Erikson, E.H. (1968) *Identity: Youth and Crisis.* New York: Norton.

Escalona, S. (1982) 'Growing up with the threat of nuclear war: Some indirect effects on personality development.' *American Journal of Orthopsychiatry 52*, 4, 600–607.

Farran, D.C. and Ramey, C.T. (1977) 'Infant day care and attachment behaviours towards mothers and teachers.' *Child Development 48*, 112–1116.

Fernald, A. and Kuhl, P.K. (1987) 'Acoustic determinants of infant preference for mothers' speech.' *Infant Behaviour and Development 10.*

Fernald, A. and Simon, T. (1984) 'Expanded intonation contours in mothers' speech to newborns.' *Developmental psychology, 20.*

Feuerstein, R. and Klein, P. (1985) 'Environmental variables and cognitive development.' In Harel and Abastaslow *The At-Risk Infant.* Baltimore: Paul H. Brookes.

Field, T. (1990) *Infancy.* Cambridge, MA: Harvard University Press.

Fischer, K.W. and Lazarson, A. (1984) *Human Development.* New York: W.H. Freeman.

Flavell, J.H. (1963) *The Developmental Psychology of Jean Piaget.* New York: Van Nostrand.

Flavell, J.H. (1971) 'Stage-related properties of cognitive development.' *Cognitive Psychology 2,* 421–453.

Flavell, J.H. (1978) 'The development of knowledge about visual perception.' In Keashey (ed) *Nebraska Symposium on Motivation.* Lincoln: University of Nebraska Press.

Flekkøy, M.G. (1989) 'Child advocacy in Norway: the Ombudsman.' *Child Welfare LXVIII,* 2, March-April.

Flekkøy, M.G. (1984) 'The Ombudsman for children: the needs of young consumers, information, communication, legislation.' *Marketing to Children and Young Consumers.* Nuremberg: ESOMAR.

Flekkøy, M.G. (1990) *Working for the Rights of Children.* Innocenti Essay no.1, Florence: ICDC/UNICEF.

Flekkøy, M.G. (1991) *Models for Monitoring the Protection of Children's Rights.* Meeting report, Florence: ICDC/UNICEF.

Flekkøy, M.G. (1991) *A Voice for Children. Speaking Out as Their Ombudsman.* London: Jessica Kingsley Publishers.

Flekkøy, M.G. (1993) 'Children's Rights. Reflections on and consequences of the use of developmental psychology in working for the interests of children. The Norwegian Ombudsman for Children: A practical experience.' Doctoral dissertation. Ghent University, Belgium.

Fortuyn, M.D. and de Langen, M. (eds) (1992) *Towards the Realization of Human Rights of Children.* Conference proceedings. Amsterdam: DCI-Netherlands.

Fox, N. (1977) 'Attachment of kibbutz infants to mother and metapelet.' *Child Development 48,* 1228–1239.

Franklin, B. (1989) 'Children's rights: developments and prospects.' *Children and Society 3,* 50–66.

Franklin, B. (1988) *Ageism and the Political Economy of Childhood.* Ghent: Studie-en Documentatie-centrum voor Rechten van Kindern cahier 6, 5–46.

Franklin, B. (ed) (1995) *The Handbook of Children's Rights. Comparative Policy and Practice.* London: Routledge.

Freeman, M.D.A. (1987–88) 'Taking children's rights seriously.' *Children and Society 4,* 299–319.

Freeman, M.D.A. (1992) 'Beyond conventions – towards empowerment.' In M.D. Fortuyn and M. de Langen (eds) *Towards the Realization of Human Rights of Children.* Amsterdam: DCI-Netherland.

Freeman, M.D.A. and Veerman, P. (eds) (1992) *Ideologies of Children's Rights.* Amsterdam: Martinus Nijhoff.

Freud, A. and Burlingham, D. (1944) *Infants without Families.* New York: International Universities Press.

Freud, A. and Dann, S. (1954) 'An experiment in group upbringing.' In W.E. Martin and C.B. Stendler (eds) *Readings in Child Development.* New York: Harcourt Brace.

Frones, I. (1987) 'On the meaning of peers.' In *Canadian Seminar on Childhood Implications for Child Care Policies.* European Centre for Social Welfare Training and Research.

Gardner, H. (1983) *Frames of Mind. The Theory of Multiple Intelligences.* New York: Basic Books.

Garvey, C. (1982) 'Communication and the development of social role play.' In D. Forbes and M.T. Grennberg (eds) *Children's Planning Strategies.* San Francisco: Jossey-Bass.

Geber, M. (1962) 'Longitudinal study and psycho-motor development among Baganda children.' In A.G. Skard and T. Husen *Child and Education. Proceedings of the XIV International Congress of Applied Psychology, Vol. III.* Copenhagen: Munksgaard.

Gilligan, C. (1982) 'New maps of development: new visions of maturity.' *American Journal of Orthopsychiaty 52,* 2.

Glaser, H.H., Hagerty, M.C. and Bullard, D.M. (1980) 'Physical and psychological development of children with early failure to thrive.' *Journal of Pediatrics 73,* 690–698.

Goldstein, J., Freud, A. and Solnit, A.J. (1973) *Before the Best Interests of the Child.* New York: Free Press.

Grant, J.P. (1991–1995) *The State of The World's Children 1991–1995.* UNICEF: Oxford University Press.

Green, E.H. (1933) 'Friendship and quarrels among preschool children.' *Child Development 4,* 237–252. In Hoffmann and Hoffmann (1964) *Review of Child Development Research Vol. 1.* New York: Russel Sage Foundation.

Gregory, I. (1958) 'Studies of parental deprivation in psychiatric patients.' *American Journal of Psychiatry 115,* 432–442.

Grieser, D.L. and Kuhl, P.K. (1988) 'Maternal speech to infants in a tonal language: support for universal prosodic features in motherese. *Developmental Psychology 24.*

Grisso, T. and Vierling, T. (1978) 'Minors' consent to treatment. A developmental perspective.' *Professional Psychology 9,* 412–427.

Hagtvedt, B.E. (1992) '"Dress" is birthday and "sleep" is night.' Young children's word definition strategies.' In A. Heen Wold (ed) *The Dialogical Alternative.* Oslo: Scandinavia University Press.

Hart, R.A. (1992) *Children's Participation. From Tokenism to Citizenship.* Florence: UNICEF, ICDC.

Hart, S.N. (1991) 'From property to person status: historical perspective on children's rights.' *American Psychologist 46*, 1, 53–59.

Heilio, P.L., Lauronen, E. and Bardy, M. (eds) (1993) *Politics of Childhood and Children at Risk. Provision-Protection-Participation.* Vienna, Eurosocial Report 45.

Hetherington, E.M., Cox, M. and Cox, R. (1978) 'The aftermath of divorce.' In H.H. Stevens Jr. and Mathews, M. (eds) *Mother/Child, Father/Child Relationships.* Washington DC: National Association for the Education of Young Children.

Hetherington, E.M., Cox, M. and Cox, R. (1982) 'Effects of divorce on parents and children.' In M. Lamb (ed) *Nontraditional Families.* Hilllsdale, NJ: Erlbaum.

Hodne, B. and Sogner, S. (1984) *Barn av sin tid.* Oslo: Universitetsforlaget.

Hoffman, L.W. (1974) 'Effects of maternal employment on the child – a review of the research.' *Developmental Psychology 10*, 204–228.

Hoffman, L.W. (1973) 'The professional woman as mother.' In *Kundsin, a Conference on Successful Women in the Sciences.* New York: Proceedings of the New York Academy of Science.

Hubley, P. and Trevarthen, C. (1979) 'Sharing a task in infancy.' In I. Uzgiris (ed) *Social Interaction During Infancy.* (New Directions for Child Development 4). San Francisco: Jossey-Bass.

Huneide, K. (1991) *Helping Disadvantaged Children.* London: Jessica Kingsley Publishers.

Huneide, K. (1988) 'Contrasting life worlds: slum children and Oslo middle-class children's world views.' In *Growing into a Modern World.* Trondheim: Conference Proceedings, Norwegian Centre for Child Research.

Jersild, A.T. and Markey, F.V. (1935) 'Conflicts between preschool children.' *Child Development Monographs 21.*

Kagan, J. (1982) 'The emergence of self.' *Journal of Child Psychology and Psychiatry 23*, 363–381.

Kagan, J., Kearsley, B. and Zelaso, P.R. (1978) *Infancy, its Place in Human Development.* Cambridge, MA: Harvard University Press.

Kempe, R.S. and Kempe, C.H. (1978) *Child Abuse.* Cambridge, MA: Harvard University Press.

Kjørholt, A.T. (1993) *Prov Selv. Kulturprosjekt og visjoner om barndom.* Trondheim: Norsk Senter for Barneforskning.

Kohlberg, L. (1968) 'The child as a moral philosopher.' *Psychology Today 2*, 4, 25–30.

Kohlberg, L. (1976) 'Moral stages and moralization.' In T. Lickona (ed) *Moral Development and Behaviour.* New York: Holt, Rinehart and Winston.

Kohn, M.L. (1963) 'Social class and parent–child relationships: an interpretation.' In S.I. Harrison and J.F. McDermott (1972) *Childhood Psychopathology. An Anthology of Basic Readings.* New York: International Universities Press.

Labov, W. (1979) 'The logic of non-standard English.' In Lee (ed) *Language Development.* New York: J.Wiley and Sons.

Landers, C. and Kagitcibasi, C. (1990) *Measuring the Psychosocial Development of Young Children*. Florence: UNICEF/ICDC.

Lansdown, G. (1995) *Taking Part. Children's Participation in Decision-Making*. London: IPRR.

Larsen, H.R. and Larsen, M. (1992) *Lyt til Børn!* Copenhagen: Det Tværministerielle Borneudvalg og Kulturministerens Arbejdsgruppe on Børn og Kultur.

Lazar, I. and Darlington, R. with Murray, H., Royce, J. and Snipper, A. (1982) 'Lasting effects of early education: A report from the consortium for longitudinal studies.' Monographs of the Society for Research in Child Development 47 (nos. 2–3, serial no. 195).

Leach, P. (1994) *Children First*. London: Michael Joseph.

Lenneberg, E.H. (1967) *The Biological Foundations of Language*. New York: Wiley.

Lewin, K.A. (1935) *A Dynamic Theory of Personality*. New York: McGraw Hill.

Lewin, K.A. (1936) *Principles of Topological Psychology*. New York: McGraw Hill.

Lewis, C. (1983) 'Decision-making related to health: when could/should children act responsibly?' In G.B. Melton, G.P. Koocher and M.J. Saks (eds) *Children's Competence to Consent*. New York: Plenum Press.

Lewis, O. (1965) 'The culture of poverty.' *Scientific American 215*, 4.

Lillestøl, K. (1994) *Porsgrunnmodellen*. Oslo: Barnog familiedepartemenhet.

Limber, S.P. and Flekkoy, M.G. 1995) 'The UN Convention on the Rights of the Child: its relevance for social scientists.' *Soc. Pol.Rep. IX*, 2.

Lippitt, R. (1940) 'An experimental study of the effect of democratic and authoritarian group atmospheres.' *Univ. la. Stud. 16*, 3, 43–198.

Lombardi, K.L. and Lapidos, E. (1990) 'Therapeutic engagements with children: integrating infant research and clinical practice.' *Psychoanalytic Psychology 7*, 1.

Maccoby, E.E. and Martin, J.A. (1983) 'Socialization in the context of the family: Parent–child interaction.' In P.H. Mussen (ed) *Handbook of Child Psychology Vol. 4* (4th ed.).

Hetherington, E.M. (ed) *Socialization, Personality, and Social Behaviour*. New York: Wiley.

Johnson, V., Hill, J and Ivan-Smith, E. (1995) *Listening to Smaller Voices: Children in an Environment of Change*. Somerset: Actionaid.

Macrae, J.W. and Herbert-Jackson, E. (1976) 'Are behavioural effects of infant day care programs specific?' *Developmental Psychology 12*, 269–270.

Mahler, M.S., Pine, F. and Bergman, A. (1975) *The Psychological Birth of the Human Infant*. New York: Basic Books.

Martin, B. (1975) 'Parent–child relations.' In F.D. Horowitz (ed) *Review of Child Development Research Vol. 4*, 463–540.

Marvin, R.S., Greenberg, M.T. and Mossler, D.G. (1976) 'The early development of conceptual perspective-taking: distinguishing among multiple perspectives.' *Child Development 47*.

Maslow, A. (1954) *Motivation and Personality*. New York: Harper and Row.

McCall, R.B., Eichorn, D.H. and Hogarty, P.S. (1977) 'Transitions in early mental development.' *Monographs of the Society for Research in Child Development 42* (3, serial no. 171).

McDermott, J.F. (1970) 'Divorce and its psychiatric sequelae in children.' *Archives of General Psychiatry 23*, 5, 421–427.

McKay,H., Sinisterra, L., McKay, A., Gomez, H. and Loreda, P. (1978) 'Improving cognitive ability in chronically deprived children.' *Science 200*, 216, 270–278.

McNeal, J.U. (1992) 'Growing up in the market.' *American Demograhics* October 1992.

Melton, G.B. (1983) *Child Advocacy*. New York: Plenum Press.

Melton, G.B. (1986) 'Populism, school prayer and the courts: confessions of an expert witness.' In D. Moshman (ed) *Children's Intellectual Rights*. San Francisco: Jossey-Bass.

Melton, G.B. (1987) 'Children, politics, and morality: the ethics of child advocacy.' *Journal of Clinical and Child Psychology 16*, 4, 357–367.

Melton, G.B. (1989) 'Respect for dignity: blueprint for children's law in the welfare state.' In *Barn 4*. Trondheim: Norsk senter for barneforskning.

Melton, G.B. (1991) 'Lessons from Norway: the children's ombudsman as a voice for children.' *Case Western Reserve Journal of Int'l Law 23*, 3.

Melton, G.B. (1991) 'Socialization in the global community.' *American Psychologist 46*, 1, 66–71.

Melton, G.B., Koocher, G.P. and Saks, M.J. (eds) (1983) *Children's Competence to Consent*. New York: Plenum Press.

Melton, G.B. and Limber, S. (1992) 'What children's rights mean to children: children's own views.' In M. Freeman and P. Veerman (eds) *Ideologies of Children's Rights*. Amsterdam: Martinus Nijhoff.

Melton, G.B. and Saks, M.J. (1985) 'The law as an instrument of socialization and social structure.' In E. Keashey (ed) *Nebraska Symposium on Motivation, 1985*. Lincoln: Nebraska University Press.

Miljeteig, P. (1994) 'Children's involvement in the implementation of their own rights – present and future perspectives.' Unpublished paper presented at the International Society for the Study of Behavioural Development 13, biannual meeting, June 28–July 1, Amsterdam.

Miljeteig-Olssen, P. (1990) 'Advocacy of children's rights – the Convention as more than a legal document.' *Human Rights Quarterly 12*, 1, 148–155.

Milne, B. (1995) 'Articles 12, 13, 14, 15, 16, and 17 of the Convention on the Rights of the Child: Participation.' *DCI National Newsletters 2*. Geneva.

Milne, B. (1995) *Children Climbing the Ladder of Participation; the Challenge of Converting Theory into Practice*. Paper presented at Progetto Bambino Urbano: I Bambini e la Strageia della Partecipazione, Milano, 13 March 1995.

Minnow, M. (1990) *Making All the Difference*. Ithaca: Cornell University Press.

Mortiman (1989) *Discipline in the Schools: Report of the Committee of Inquiry Chaired by Lord Elton*. London: DES.

Moshman, D. (ed) (1986) *Children's Intellectual Rights*. San Francisco: Jossey-Bass.

Moshman, D. (1989) *Children, Education and the First Amendment.* Lincoln: University of Nebraksa Press.

Murphy, L.B. (1937) *Social Behavior and Child Personality.* New York: Columbia University Press.

Murray, L. and Trevarthen, C. (1985) 'Emotion regulation of interaction between two month olds and their mothers.' In T.M. Field and N. Fox (eds) *Social Perceptions in Infants.* New Jersey: Ablex.

Mussen, P.H., Conger J.J. and Kagan, J. (1963) *Child Development and Personality* 2nd ed. New York: Harper and Row.

Nagel, J. (1987) *Participation.* Englewood, NJ: Prentice-Hall.

Nissen, M. (1985) *Skilsmisse og Børn.* Copenhagen: Socialforsknings-instituttet.

Oates, R.K., Peacock, A. and Forrest, D. (1984) 'Development in children following abuse and nonorganic failure to thrive.' *American Journal of Diseases in Children 138,* 764–767.

Ogden, T., Backe-Hansen, E. and Kristofersen, L. (1994) *Barn og Unges Sosiale Kompetanse.* Oslo: Prosjekt Oppvekstnettverk.

Olweus, D. (1984/1988) 'School as a context for social development.' In *Child Research in Norway.* Trondheim: NAVF Centre for Child Research.

Papalia, D.E. and Olds, S.W. (1981) *Human Development,* 2nd ed. New York: McGraw-Hill.

Papousek, M. (1987) 'Models and messages in the melodies of maternal speech in tonal and non-tonal languages.' *Abstracts of Society for Research in Child Development 6.*

Parker, S., Greer, S. and Zuckerman, B. (1988) 'Double jeopardy: the impact of poverty on early child development.' *Pediatric Clinics of North America 35,* 6, 1227–1240.

Pateman, C. (1970) *Participation and Democratic Theory.* New York: Cambridge University Press.

Piaget, J. (1952) *The Origin of Intelligence in Children.* New York: Norton.

Piaget, J. (1955) *The Moral Judgement of the Child.* New York: Macmillan.

Provence, S. and Lipton, R. (1962) *Infants in Institutions.* New York: International Universities Press.

Prugh, D.G., Staub, E., Sands, H., Kirschbaum, R. and Lenihan, E. (1952) 'A study of the emotional reactions of children and families to hospitalization and illness.' *American Journal of Orthopsychiatry 23,* 70–106.

Pugh, G. and Selleck, D.R. (1995) 'Listening to and communicating with young children.' In Davie, Upnor and Varner (eds) *The Voice of the Child: a Handbook for Professionals.* Fodner Press.

Qvortrup, J. (1990) *Childhood as a Social Phenomenon – an Introduction to a Series of National Reports.* Eurosocial Reports Series no. 36, Vienna: European Centre for Social Welfare Policy and Research.

Qvortrup, J. (1993) *Barndom – en ny minoritet? Nordisk barndom i et samfundsperspektiv.* Esbjerg: Sydjydsk Universitetscenter.

Qvortrup, J. (1996) 'Monitoring childhood: its social, economic and political features.' In Verhallen, E. (ed) *Monitoring Children's Rights*. The Hague: Martinus Nijhoff Publishers.

Raundalen, M. (1983) *Skremmeskudd*. Oslo: Universitetsforlaget.

Raundalen, M. and Raundalen, T.S. (1984) *Barn i atomalderen*. Oslo: Cappelen.

Rosenheim, M.K. 'The child and the Law.' In B. Caldwell and H.N. Ricciuti (1973) *Review of Child Development Research, Vol. 3*. Chicago: The University of Chicago Press.

Rouse, D. (1992) *The Italian Experience*. London: National Children's Bureau (unpub.)

Rubenstein, J.L. and Howes, C. (1979) 'Caregiving and infant behavior in day care and in homes.' *Developmental Psychology 15*, 1–24.

Rudberg, M. (1983) *Dydige, sterke, lykkelige barn*. Oslo: Universitetsforlaget.

Ruiz-Gimenez, J. (1989) 'The development of the rights of the child.' *Children Worldwide 16*, 3, 12–14.

Rutter, M. (1971) 'Parent–child separation: psychological effects on the children.' *Journal of Child Psychology and Psychiatry 12*, 233–260.

Rutter, M. (1978) 'Early sources of security and competence.' In J. Bruner and A. Garten (eds) *Human Growth and Development*. London: Oxford University Press.

Rutter, M. (1979a) *Fifteen Thousand Hours: Secondary Schools and Their Effects on Pupils*. London: Open Books.

Rutter, M. (1979b) 'Separation experiences: A new look at an old topic.' *Pediatrics 95*, 1, 147–154.

Rutter, M. (1987) 'Psychosocial resilience and protective mechanisms.' *American Journal of Orthopsychiatry 57*, 316–331.

Rutter, M. and Madge, N. (1976) *Cycles of Disadvantage*. Kingston: Heinemann Educational Books.

Schwebel, M. (1982) 'Effects of nuclear war threat on children and teenagers: implications for professionals.' *American Journal of Orthopsychiatry 52*, 4, 608–618.

Scribner, S. and Cole, M. (1981) *The Consequences of Literacy*. Cambridge, MA: Harvard University Press.

Sears, R.R., Maccoby, E.E. and Levin, H. (1957) *Patterns of Child Rearing*. New York: Harper and Row.

Seip Flaaten, E. and Sandbæk, M. (1981) *Barnevern – barnas vern?* Oslo: Oslo barnevernkontor.

Seligman, M.E.P. (1975) *Helplessness*. San Francisco: W.H. Freeman.

Selman, R.L. (1976) 'Social-cognitive understanding: a guide to educational and clinical practice.' In T. Lickona (ed) *Moral Development and Behavior*. New York: Holt, Rinehart and Winston.

Shugar, G.W. (1988) 'The nature of peer discourse: participant structures for and by children.' In R. Søderbergh (ed) *Children's Creative Communication*. Lund: Lund University Press.

Sigsgaard, E. (1979) *Om børn og deres virkelighed*. Copenhagen: Hans Reitzel.

Silva, K. (1984) Nurturing play in a cold economic climate. Keynote address, IPA Conference India 1983 in *IPA Newsletter*, April.

Silva, K., Roy, C. and Genova, P. (1980) *Childwatching at Playgroups and Nursery School.* London: McIntyre.

Silva, K., Bruner, J.S. and Genova, P. (1976) 'The role of play in the problem-solving of children 3–5 years old.' In J. Bruner *et al.* (eds) *Play: its Role in Development and Evolution.* London: Penguin.

Skard, Å.G. (1981) 'Det imperative "nei".' In *Norsk Pedagogisk Tidsskrift* no. 1 (reprinted in English, *The Imperative No, The Delta Cappa Gamma Bulletin* 48, 1982 no. 4, 17– 24.

Skard, Å.G. (1965) 'Maternal deprivation: the research and its implications.' *Journal of Marriage and the Family 27,* 333–343.

Staub, E. (1971) 'The use of role-playing and induction in children's learning of helping and sharing behavior.' *Child Development 42,* 805–816.

Stern, D. (1974) 'Mother and infant at play: the dyadic interaction involving facial, vocal and gaze behaviors.' In M. Lewis and L. Rosenblum (eds) *The Effect of the Infant on its Caregiver.* New York: John Wiley.

Stern, D. (1974) 'The goal and structure of mother–infant play.' *Journal of the American Academy of Child Psychiatry 13,* 402–421.

Stern, D. (1985) *The Interpersonal World of the Infant. A View from Psychoanalysis and Developmental Psychology.* New York: Basic Books.

Stevenson, H.W. (1982) 'Influences of schooling on cognitive development.' In D.A. Wagner and H.W. Stevenson (eds) *Cultural Perspectives on Child Development.* San Francisco: W.H. Freeman.

Stoch, M., Smythe, P. and Moodie, A. (1982) 'Psychosocial outcome and CT findings after gross undernourishment during infancy. A 20-year developmental study.' *Developmental Medicine and Child Neurology 24,* 419–436.

Stone, L. (1977) *The Family, Sex and Marriage in England 1500–1800.* New York: Harper and Row. Quoted in S. Hart (1991) From property to person status. In *American Psychologist 46,* 1, 53–59.

Thomas, A. and Chess, S. (1977) *Temperament and Development.* New York: Brunner Mazel.

Tiller, P.O. (1983) 'Barnsmedvirkning i forskning om barns levekår.' In *Barn. Nytt fra forskning om barn i Norge.* Trondheim: Senter for Barneforskning.

Tizard, B. (1977) *Adoption: A Second Chance.* London: Open Books.

Tønnessen, L.K. (1982) *Slik levde småbarna før.* Oslo: Universitetsforlaget.

Trevarthen, C. (1977) 'Descriptive analyses of infant communication behaviour.' In H.R. Schaffer (ed) *Studies in Mother–Infant Interaction: The Loch Lomond Symposium.* London: Academic Press.

Trevarthen, C. (1992) 'An infant's motives for speaking and thinking.' In A. Heen Wold. *The Dialogical Alternative. Towards a Theory of Language and Mind.* Oslo: Scandinavian University Press.

Van Bueren, G. (1994) *Children's Access to Adoption Records – State Discretion or an Enforceable International Right?* Unpublished paper presented at Wild Dunes S.C. Seminar on The Child's Right to a Family, organized by the Institute for Families in Society.

Verhellen, E. (1990) *Changing in Child-images. Reflections in National and International (draft) Rules and Jurisdiction in Europe.* Paper presented at The first International Interdisciplinary Study-group on Ideologies of Children's Rights, Israel (mimeo).

Verhellen, E. (1993) 'Children and participation rights.' In P.L. Heilio, E. Lauronen and M. Bardy. *Politics of Childhood and Children at Risk. Provision-Protection-Participation.* Vienna, Eurosocial Report 45.

Verhellen, E. and Spiesschaert, F. (eds) (1989) *Ombudswork for Children.* Leuven: Acco (Academic Publishing Company).

Verhellen, E. (eds) (1994) *Children's Rights: Monitoring Issues.* Ghent: Mys and Breesch.

Vestby, G.M. and Solberg, A. *Barns arbeidsliv.* Oslo: NIBR-rapport 1987:3.

Wallerstein, J.S. and Kelly, J.B. (1980) *Surviving the Breakup: How Children and Parents Cope with Divorce.* New York: Basic Books.

Weikart, D. (1989) 'The High/Scope Perry Preschool Study: implications for early childhood care and education.' *Prevention in Human Service 7, 1.*

Weikart, D., Epstein, A.S., Schweinhart, L. and Bond, J.T. (1978) *The Ypsilanti Preschool Curriculum and Demonstration Project: Preschool Years and Longitudinal Results.* Ypsilanti, MI: High/Scope Educational Research Foundation.

Weithorn, L.A. (1980) *Competency to Render Informed Treatment Decisions: A Comparison Between Certain Minors and Adults.* Unpublished doctoral dissertation, University of Pittsburgh.

Weithorn, L.A. (1983) 'Involving children in decisions affecting their own welfare: guidelines for professionals.' In G.B. Melton, G.P. Koocher and M.J. Saks (eds) *Children's Competence to Consent.* New York: Plenum Press.

Werner, H. (1948) *Comparative Psychology of Mental Development.* Chicago: Follett.

White, R. (1959) 'Motivation reconsidered: the concept of competence.' *Psychological Review 66,* 297–33.

Whiting, B.B. and Whiting, J.W.M. (1975) *Children of Six Cultures: a Psycho-cultural Analysis.* Cambridge, MA: Harvard University Press.

Whiting, B.B. and Edwards (1988) *Children of Different Worlds.* Cambridge, MA: Harvard University Press.

Wikan, U. (1985) 'Barn og straff.' Trondheim: NAVF,SfB, rapport nr. 6.

Wikan, U. (1976) *Fattigfolk i Kairo.* Oslo: Gyldendal Norsk Forlag.

Subject Index

References in italic indicate figures or tables.

Author Index